GATHERING

A WOMEN WHO SUBMIT ANTHOLOGY

FICTION EDITORS
Ryane Nicole Granados
Lorinda Toledo

NONFICTION EDITORS
Noriko Nakada
Flint

DRAMA EDITORS
Xochitl-Julisa Bermejo
Sharnell Blevins

POETRY EDITORS
Lauren Eggert-Crowe
Lituo Huang

MANAGING EDITOR
Tisha Marie Reichle-Aguilera

Gathering: A Women Who Submit Anthology

Jamii Publishing

Jamii Publishing
Santa Cruz, CA
www.jamiipublishing.com
[clmp]

Front Cover Design: Rachael Warecki
NOTE: Three of Wands in tarot is a symbol of both community and of creative writers/freelancers

Back Cover and Interior Design: Tisha Marie Reichle-Aguilera and Rachael Warecki

Managing Editor: Tisha Marie Reichle-Aguilera
Copy Editor: Xochitl-Julisa Bermejo

Production: Nikia Chaney, Cynthia Manick, Emily Blair

Library of Congress Cataloging-in-Publishing Data

ISBN: 978-1-7332415-4-0

Dedicated to the memory of
Natalie Smith Parra (1958-2021)

and all the women and nonbinary writers
who left us during this time.

ACKNOWLEDGEMENTS

This anthology was made possible by a grant from Eastside Arts Initiative, sponsorship by Antioch University Los Angeles, the generosity of individual donors, and the fiscal sponsorship of Avenue 50 Studio.

This publication could not exist without the generosity and collaboration of Nikia Chaney at Jamii Publishing.

Thank you to all the chapter leads across the country who continue to gather and support the submission efforts of our members.

GATHERING was also inspired by:

Joy Harjo
Cherríe Moraga
Audre Lorde
Jeanette LeBlanc
Toni Morrison
Starhawk
bell hooks
Alice Waters
Amanda Gorman
Gloria Anzaldúa
Lorraine Hansberry
Sandra Cisneros
Ntozake Shange

Women Who Submit was created in response to the 2010 VIDA Count. We are grateful to VIDA: Women in Literary Arts for their inspiration and commitment to creating transparency around the lack of gender parity in the literary landscape and to amplifying historically-marginalized voices, including people of color; writers with disabilities; and queer, trans and gender nonconforming individuals. (www.vidaweb.org)

CONTENTS

FICTION

CREATIVE NONFICTION

DRAMA

POETRY

Historically, pandemics have forced humans to break with the past and imagine their world anew. This one is no different. It is a portal, a gateway between one world and the next. We can choose to walk through it, dragging the carcasses of our prejudice and hatred, our avarice, our data banks and dead ideas, our dead rivers and smoky skies behind us. Or we can walk through lightly, with little luggage, ready to imagine another world. And ready to fight for it.

- Arundhati Roy, "The Pandemic is a Portal"
in *Financial Times*, April 3, 2020

FOREWORD

Kitchen Table Revelry

by TISHA MARIE REICHLE-AGUILERA

In "Perhaps the World Ends Here," Joy Harjo opens with "The world begins at a kitchen table." That is how Women Who Submit began. I was invited to share snacks and submit my fiction to literary journals at Xochitl-Julisa Bermejo's parents' kitchen table. We gathered to empower one another, share struggles and resources, to ultimately form a supportive community of women writers.

For the past ten years, Women Who Submit (WWS) has done that and more. We created safe, nurturing spaces in Los Angeles first, refined our goals, and together created a vision for embracing other women and nonbinary writers. The WWS leadership team has created programs, garnered funding, and presented at conferences. In 2015-2016, I attended more than 10 writing conferences and workshops in seven different cities to share WWS's mission through submission strategy workshops and in social settings. Now, WWS has more than 27 chapters across the US, one in Mexico, and we continue to grow. WWS members gathered at kitchen and café tables, in bars and libraries, in art galleries and community spaces, in each other's homes and on back patios—always with the goal of expanding our literary community. Because of WWS, I developed the confidence needed to apply for editorial positions, fellowships, and a PhD program.

In 2020, WWS celebrated members' submissions with our first anthology, *ACCOLADES.* It had a gorgeous cover designed by Rachael Warecki and was featured in CLMP's Year-End Roundup of anthologies. We had a release party at AWP in San Antonio and when the coronavirus threatened our physical safety, members read their work in virtual settings. There were

Instagram takeovers and livestreamed readings, weekly check-ins and Writing Alone Together in multiple time zones. We gathered online to encourage one another to keep writing, keep submitting, and keep supporting each other through traumatic times.

The world did not end, but it has been forever altered. Through it all, we scribbled and typed, danced and sang, laughed and cried, baked and ate, crocheted and crafted, read in silence and shouted out frustrations when necessary. Joy Harjo calls the kitchen table "a place to hide in the shadow of terror. A place to celebrate the terrible victory."

That is what we as writers must continue doing: persevere when we can, rest when we need it, and revel in the moments of joy that words can give us. This anthology is a testament to all the ways we have endured the past year, the ways our writing and our writing community have sustained and inspired us. Women Who Submit will continue to gather in small groups and as a global community so that our voices can be heard, and our words can be shared.

Ahoy, Women Who Submit: A collaborative poem-map launched at dawn of the pandemic in Women Who Submit's Saturday Virtual Check-in

by MELISSA CHADBURN, DÉSIRÉE ZAMORANO, XOCHITL-JULISA BERMEJO, LISA EVE CHEBY, DARIA TOPOUSIS, FLINT, AMANDA L. ANDREI, COLETTE SARTOR, SHARNELL BLEVINS, VK LYNNE, CYBELE GARCIA KOHEL, CARLA SAMETH, LISBETH COIMAN, VALERIE BURNS, NORIKO NAKADA

curated by HAZEL KIGHT WITHAM

Ahoy (as used on ships) was used as the first telephone greeting. Back in 1889, central telephone exchange operators were known as 'hello-girls' because of the association between the greeting and the telephone.

Ahoy, Women Who Submit~
These mornings sinking
under the weight of extraordinary
now rendered ordinary

Today,
I made coffee
wondering if I should save a cup for our time together.
I cut fruit, read through my journal, wrote new words.
This is how I prepared for you.

This how I remember I am real,
we are connected,
and time is sacred.

This, our respite: a brief breath of rest
relief from sea of sorrow
from Latin *respectus*: 'refuge, consideration'.

How we respect us
streaming through the torrents
we are sail and propeller and rudder
we are this blessed wind
guiding us through storm
this respite becomes refuge from inertia

I thought I wasn't worthy
But you left a window cracked for me, and I slipped
through guiltily,
prepared to sit quietly in a corner.
Instead, you invited me into the circle,
you poured me a drink,
and you made me realize that I never really left.

Ahoy, Hello-Girls/Women/Badass/Feminist/Womanist/
Touchstones~

We, Touchstones: assaying tool,
to *assay*—to try, endeavor, strive
to *essay*—to experiment, venture

Even just writing this
is movement, breath—inward, outward, through.

Together, inside respite, we remember:
Writing is the solace, the struggle,
the shadow and the light,
this breath that always matters.

You let me clear my throat.
You let me stretch my hands.

Listen—someone is unmuted.
I hear birds chirping
from their room into mine.

Over 225 days
This space has been
map to new world that came barreling in
without invitation, without instructions

until we, Ahoy-Women,
we, Touchstones, began cartography together

mapping:
accomplishments: to celebrate, to commemorate
goals: where are you voyaging next, where will your words go?
needs: how can we star-spell each other through?

After living years isolated,
through too much trauma,
depression, loss of hope,
I'm now a member of this crew of
accomplished, bright, powerful, formidable women.

Ahoy, Girls~
Come here, to this mosaic of women,
land somewhere that keeps celebrating,
keeps centering,
keeps keeping us whole.

Ahoy, Touchstones~

you remind me of the times that I have fallen
in love with me
with what I am supposed to be
Me
all of me
every bit of me
These Saturday morning jaunts
forever recenter me

in the things that
fill my soul
my writing
redirects my soul

These cells are breath and music and joy.
Marking the weeks,
mapping pages and poems and possibility.
During a year intent on anchoring all our levity
we joy and promise and ask
all sail and propeller and rudder and wind
guiding us through storm.

This time
a blessing
I am learning, finally
to carve out my own existence
an annex for my self
me alone
through community,
through shared space,
seeing front page value
where I once only saw margins

Ahoy, Community~
collecting on solitary days
Women, power, strength
Words bleed from heavy eyes
Words exhale from tired lungs
Words wind out from spools on our tongues,
float in the air from one vessel to the next,
binding us together, making us powerful.

Ahoy, Women~

Before this, Saturday mornings were a zone of loss,
the loose change of my mind
unspent, squandered.

But now: behold the riches,
the richness that sustains and carries
during the week away,
we write words and bon-voyage them into the world
to map their own way, find their own home.

This group galvanizes
as lockdown lengthens
and anxiety heightens.
I would have mired myself
in the worsening news of the world

But this group:
strong, devoted, determined, wildly talented women
has kept me focused and settled.
Has allowed me to remember
the joy of creation,
the power of it; the necessity.

A structure for the confined lives of
unshowered writers no longer adrift
gathering to manifest intentions
snapping fingers, jazzing hands,
Waving off anxiety pooling inside
sweaty masks, latex gloves,
Holding accountability through
despair and uncertainty

Tears washed by dark coffee, boldly
laced with hope
acknowledging land and losses,
uprising and revolution

Ahoy, Women~

Even while I stumble over these words of gratitude,
let's just say mil gracias and love
for all this space has given me, us

Ahoy, Women~
Look how we make land together
map these discouraging, divided times
make community across wonder of air
buoy and breath in these high seas
safe haven, respite,
touchstone and life-line
as we sail our words out

to map something new.

If we could make this connection in our heart of hearts, if we are serious about a revolution, if we seriously believe there should be joy in our lives, then we need one another. The real power ... is collective. This polite timidity is killing us.

Cherríe Moraga

Welcome to my TED Talk: A Monologue About Work/Life Balance

by RYANE NICOLE GRANADOS

This is a tale about teeth. It's also a saga about a mom in the middle of a pandemic juggling children, a writing career, and working against a deadline. But mostly it's just about teeth...and cheeseburgers!

RYANE

The baby has been fussy for some days now, but the pediatrician assures me it's too early for her to be teething. Yet what do I find poking through her gums? The bud of a tooth. My teenager is on a hunger strike because we did the unthinkable and got him braces. We figured when he had straight teeth, he would thank us later. For now he is threatening to never smile again. And then there's our 7-year old with teeth dangling all throughout his mouth. He is our future financier. He's obsessed with money from the tooth fairy so he keeps talking about elaborate plans to rip his teeth out. One strategy even includes tying a string to a remote controlled car. We typically disregard most of his jawing because out of all of our children he has the lowest pain threshold of all. But on this day, the deadline day to turn in a submission for publication, I just need a few uninterrupted hours. At this point I'm willing to find him the string. Hell, I might dig out the RC car too. Recently I've been battling my own toothache, followed by a root canal, and an eventual back tooth extraction. It seems pregnancy strips the calcium off of your teeth. The dentist gave me a temporary tooth implant, but I mostly use it to yell at the kids, "If you don't listen I'm going to take my tooth out." They seem to get a kick out of this stunt. So I move from room to room, writing, moving, writing, dodging all while wearing a baby strapped to my chest. Periodically, I remove my tooth retainer upon request from the envious 7-year old. Then I decide to order fast food because even cooking dinner is going to cost me valuable writing hours. The kids agree on cheeseburgers as the teenager is finally starved enough to eat. I nibble fries in between editing. And then it happens! I can hear a loud scream, but not one of those someone-just-injured-themselves-and-we-will-spend-the-rest-of-the-night-in-the-ER type of scream; more of a squeal of pure delight. My 1st grader's tooth has finally fallen out thanks to a monster bite into his burger. His joy is palpable. Even the teenager gifts me a smile showing a mouth full of braces. Eager to please the tooth fairy, my little moneybags has gone to bed early. The baby seemingly picking up on the trend falls asleep too. I may meet the deadline after all and just in time to remind my husband to bring home cash to slide under our son's pillow. I guess my work/ life balance strategy is not much of a strategy at all: sometimes it's just giving yourself enough grace to order Five Guys for dinner.

Había Una Vez

by DÉSIRÉE ZAMORANO

from *CRAB CREEK REVIEW*

Whenever his mother served him a plate of food, he would find a strand of her hair.

How she apologized! How his father laughed! How she stroked his face and kissed the top of his head! He then would uncomplainingly remove the strand of hair, drop it to the floor, wipe his hands, then eat his breakfast of migas: eggs scrambled with fried tortillas. Or lunch of bean tacos. Or dinner of enchiladas. His mother's hair, a stray wisp, a strand, sometimes an eyelash, accompanied her food for him.

His father was no longer there. Why? Had he said goodbye? The boy could not remember. Where had he gone? When would he be back? His mother's answers were vague: soon, soon.

His mother served rice and beans, rice and beans, (and a slip of her hair) rice and beans. Then, later, corn tortillas. Just tortillas. Corn tortillas and salt.

He did not know for how long they only ate corn tortillas and salt. One morning, he watched his mother gather clothes and water and food into a cloth and fold it all together. She gathered a smaller bundle for him to carry.

They walked. He held her hand and watched brightly colored birds fly overhead. They walked and he was farther away from his home than he had ever been. They walked on dry roads, through green passageways. They moved for cars. A family offered them a ride, and that was his first time in a car. They ended up in an enormous city, it seemed to him, with people and buildings and noises and sounds that never ended, that went on forever and ever. There were streetlights and lighted buildings at night.

They slept in a bus station and waited with who-knew-how-many other people. The people seemed, like the city, to spread and go on forever. His mother carefully unwrapped the tortillas she had packed and there, of course, was a strand of her hair on the tip of his tongue. He gently removed it and munched on the dry, salted tortilla. He went with her to buy water.

A woman his mother had been speaking to held their place in line. His mother took him by the hand and pulled him into a room with a sink and a trickle of water. She had him use the stall, and then she rinsed a cloth she had been carrying. She washed his face, his hands, scrubbed his body part by part. She rinsed out the cloth again with soap she had brought from home. He watched her scrub her face, her neck, her arms, her body, bit by bit, then scrub the cloth again.

They left the washroom. When they returned to the line, the woman gave them a papaya and an avocado. His mother put them in her bag. The people spoke softly about the army. The people spoke softly about the rebels.

"Both sides burn our villages," an old man muttered.

The woman said, "Hush!!!!"

In the morning when they got on the bus, he sat on his mother's lap.

The ride was exciting! The went high in the hills, nearly touching clouds. He looked into the eyes of a bird flying by them; as the bus creaked upwards, the bodies of the passengers fell back and heavily into their seats. They made slow and breathless turns and at one point all the passengers shrieked, and then they headed slowly downwards, past dry landscape, then into verdant greenery then deep into the level valley floor. It was night, and he could see no more. He and his mother slept.

When the bus stopped, everyone awoke. The sky was a color he had never seen before, it was as if smoke shrouded the sun. Everyone clambered out of the bus and went in their own directions.

He and his mother stood outside the bus station, watching the soldiers pass with their guns slung on their shoulders. The soldiers did not look at them.

His mother gave him a tortilla mashed with avocado. He was suddenly surrounded by tiny birds who pecked at the ground at his feet. Their eyes looked sad and ravenous. He felt his stomach rumble, but he said nothing.

He tore his food into small bits and fed the birds.

"Why did you do that?" his mother asked, angry with him.

"They looked so hungry," he said.

She shook her head. "You may be that way soon."

The day grew brighter, behind the shroud of smoke. The boots of many soldiers rumbled past them. Man after man, dressed in green and black, wearing helmets, their guns slung across their shoulders, or held ready in front of them. They did not look left or right, they marched or jogged forward, forward. He watched his mother bite her lip.

"No one will come for us today," she said to him. "We should have gone with the others," she shook her head. "Now we must walk alone."

The way she said that frightened him, and he began to cry.

She picked him up and held him to her arms. "Not now, my boy, not now." She gave him the papaya. He held it in his hands.

They walked slowly, in the direction the soldiers had gone. Thick, gnarled tree roots spread across the path.

"Be careful, son. Let us honor these trees, and thank them for their shade and their existence by avoiding their roots. How would you feel if people stepped on your toes?"

She smiled and he laughed, and the two of them stepped carefully around the thick knotted veins that threaded the pathway.

They traveled up, paused. From a hilltop they could see the line of soldiers snaking forward, forward, and smoke in the distance. It was then his mother wavered. She stopped, uncertain. They turned.

Their volcano puffed, gently, softly, tufts of white clouds escaping from its spout. It looked so much closer now. It had been so far away when they started out.

He was so tired! He was so hungry! But he knew his mother knew all this already. He said nothing.

They sat, and his mother scooped out the black seeds and sliced the papaya. Above them came an immediate chittering. Monkeys! Dozens of lithe, black-armed monkeys looked down at them, chattered through their pink lips, patted their white chests.

"Shoo!" his mother said, and the monkeys laughed at them, showered leaves and seeds before scattering.

They sat down to eat their slices of papaya. He ate, and juice spilled down his cheeks, his hands. His mother had finished hers and closed her eyes. He had one luscious slice left when he noticed a somber and silent monkey, its hair completely gray, watching him. He approached it, and held out his last slice of fruit.

The monkey grabbed the food and scampered away.

They walked away from the soldiers, away from town. There was no more path. Soon his mother carried him, and he fell asleep, feeling her heart against his chest.

It was cold when he awoke, in a small room with a tiny window he could not reach, and his mother nowhere. He tried the door. Locked. He called out. Silence.

There was a cold plate of food on the floor near the door. He ate it, but first pulled out a strand of hair. Delicate, yet strong.

His mother had cooked this food. Where was she?

A tiny bird flew through the window and pecked at the sauce

left on his plate.

It looked up at him. "Keep the strands of hair," it said. "Wrap them around your wrist."

The boy nodded.

For the next thirty days the boy shivered alone, eating the sole plate of food set out for him. A man with a gun slung over his shoulder brought the food in the morning; another man with a gun over his shoulder emptied the bucket of waste at night. Neither of the men answered his questions, or spoke to him, or looked at him.

After thirty days, he had a thick collection of hair.

The bird returned. "Make a braid with the hair, and use it as a belt around your waist. Keep one strand in your hand."

The bird watched the boy as he did as he was told. When he finished, the bird said, "Good." The bird picked up the strand of hair, flew to the door, fished the hair in the lock, and said, "Follow me."

The boy trailed the bird, who flitted from lantern to lantern, then stopped in an opening, then continued left. Again the bird used the hair to fish the lock of the door. When the boy pushed it forward, there was his father! Sleeping.

The boy ran to his father and prodded him with his hands. His father awoke with round, surprised eyes, hugged his son. His father's arms were thicker than the boy remembered, his hands rough and calloused.

"We must keep going," the bird said.

His father said, "I know where she is."

This time the bird and the boy trailed the father as he swept through corridor after corridor until he stopped at a locked door.

Again, the bird used the hair to fish the lock of the door.

The boy rushed to his mother, put his arms around her sleeping body, then murmured into her ear, "We must go, quietly, now." His mother's eyes opened with delight and surprise and worry. Without a sound, she lifted herself up from the mat and, along with her son and her husband, followed the bird.

It was very early in the morning, the air cool and damp, and the sun still far away and grey.

"I know where to go," she said,

"Go," said the bird. And to the boy, "But remember your belt, and throw it down when you feel you have no choice."

The bird dipped its head and flew off.

They walked through the kitchen, as silently as possible. The boy felt the cool outside air and saw thick trees in the distance. Could they get there? Could they run fast enough? The sounds of others pounded toward the kitchen.

In through the windows and the outer door swept dozens of monkeys, who picked up pots and knives. The old grey monkey prodded a wooden spoon at the fire, just as the boy's mother and father grabbed the boy's hands. They ran, they fled, toward the grove of trees.

The boy looked back and the building they had just left was on fire; dozens of monkeys ran out and scattered into other directions. A troop of gun-shouldering soldiers ran rhythmically toward the boy and his family.

"Now!" the bird chirruped.

The boy loosened the belt made of braided hair and flung it to the ground.

The hair unfurled, each strand spanning the pathway. As the soldiers stomped on the hair, the hair wrapped itself around their ankles and legs. All of them tripped onto the ground and lay hacking away at the indestructible hair.

As the boy and his family ran toward the grove, his father said, "They needed a laborer."

His mother said, "They needed a cook. Later, I am sure they would make you fight for them."

"Were they soldiers or rebels?" the boy asked.

"They were men with guns," she answered.

Had you been watching from the burning compound you

would have seen the trio run into the grove of trees, step carefully to avoid the thick exposed roots. Once the family disappeared from sight, you would have seen the limbs and branches of the trees outstretch, intertwining to create a dense, impenetrable barricade behind the fleeing family.

Without community, there is no liberation, only the most vulnerable and temporary armistice between the individual and her oppression. But community must not mean a shedding of our differences, nor the pathetic pretense that these differences do not exist.

Audre Lorde

Shikata Ga Nai

by SAKAE MANNING

from *TAHOMA LITERARY REVIEW*

My mother died in the time of pandemic, on a morning when fires raged all over California, and smoke was choking her garden into dust. George Floyd was already murdered. Breonna Taylor's murder was going unanswered. Americans of all races and ages took to the streets to protest 400 years of systemic racism and injustice. A reality TV host was running the country. I'm left to wonder if she knew what was happening outside her house set in the foothills bordering the Sierra Nevada and only miles from where Mark Twain made frog jumping famous. By now, her eyes were failing, making running impossible.

My mother died on a Tuesday; the first of September. She secretly liked being first, so the date seemed fitting. The coroner described it as a sudden and catastrophic death. A massive heart attack or a stroke. She had spent ninety years running, putting others' needs in front of her own, hiding from bombs that echoed inside her long after the war was over. She found a way to freedom in a wavy-haired, Oklahoma-born merchant marine. A big talker. A smart man who claimed salt air and the open sea were his home. She straightened and cut her hair like Audrey Hepburn, rouged her full lips into a pout. She came to America, believing she could be American, but the ground never felt like home. The food, the language, the people—as foreign as a sliver of glass lost in the flat part of her small foot.

If she were here, my mother would say hers was a good death. Not even her head touched the ground. The crossing to join her ancestors was quick. Much easier than when she traveled on a freightliner twelve years after the war ended. My father said it was cheaper than travel on a passenger ship. She'd be fine, he decided, without considering comfort or that she couldn't speak English. My mother was locked in a lower-level room without a window. She was, after all, an alien, a lingering reminder of a war that kicked-off in Pearl Harbor. Seasickness overwhelmed her. She tossed and turned on her cot, losing weight, wondering about a widowed mother and four siblings left without an older sister. In that small dark room, normally used for storage, my mother's starched traveling dress hung from a hook on the door, swinging with the pitching ship, wilting from humidity. For two weeks, a bucket was her constant companion until the freightliner pulled into San Francisco. Her hope waned, as cargo unloaded before she could step foot on shore.

My father finally rushed up to receive her, pointing out the Golden Gate Bridge, as she stood on the pier, queasy, following his finger traveling along the horizon. San Francisco filled her lungs, reminding her of Yokohama. They drove inland, traveling north on a highway bordered by pastures and grazing cattle, empty hills with swaying grasses, and passing freight trains crawling on long, curved tracks towards Oakland. They drove into Suisun City, a small rough looking town dotted with pool halls, bars, and farmhands loitering around neon-lit liquor stores. My father pointed out the market where she would shop, the high school he had attended, the butcher he liked, but her English wasn't good enough to understand. All she heard was pride.

My mother's heart knew there was no point in trying to tell him this is not what he promised. She said there was no going back when you marry an American so learned to hide inside herself, in a mind wound so tight, she hardly slept. She feared America even more when he gave her a baby; then, another eleven months later. They knotted her future to this man. A woman running in circles, a baby on each hip, weighing her down, with nowhere to go.

My mother died, having never told my brother what she wanted—not her dreams, nor her death wishes. She told stories once. There were no repeats like people do when they get older, forget what happened yesterday, or run out of things to talk about. It was on the listener to remember, because if asked about the story, she denied ever having the conversation. I learned to pay attention when she was catching her breath from all the running.

She told me she had not wanted to marry a Japanese man and have a foot on her neck for the rest of her life. I responded, "So you came here and had a foot on your back instead?" She triple blinked, her mouth a line so tight a fine needle, the kind used to sew organza or chiffon, couldn't slip in. Her fingers went back to pinning a tissue pattern to an emerald green bolt of taffeta. That's what my mother did; she made fancy dresses for rich wives of government officials, for weddings, and for quinceañeras. The latter made my mother most happy, because she ended up making sixteen gowns, fourteen in the same design, one for the quinceañera, and one for the mother celebrating her daughter's entry into womanhood. The girl in white tulle and satin, put on display for all to admire, to set her up for a life in patriarchy.

My mother understood the patriarchy, living with a husband who controlled her every move. She said she liked being a second class citizen, infuriating my brother, and entrusting men to make decisions for her. Except for the dollar amount, my father signed checks before she went grocery shopping. The cashier wrote in the amount. She walked in rain or triple-digit heat, four long blocks with a full grocery cart, while my father smoked his pipe or napped at home. All credit cards were in his name, so she requested and he pre-approved all purchases whether it was a pair of shoes or a pack of underwear. My mother understood the cost of staying in America, of saving face.

She's gone now, my mother. My brother said her glasses remained on her face. Her hair in place; wispy at the neckline.

The Buddhist priest chanted prayers here, in Los Angeles, while her body cooled on a table at the coroner's up north in Gold Rush country. For Shinto, the body should never be separated from the prayers, nor from its sacred departure rituals, but that's what happens when living on strange ground, a former mining town where Chinese were lynched. When my parents moved there, I warned her, most Americans can't tell the difference between Chinese and Japanese, and she laughed.

She was used to being the only one, alone in a country where she had no mother, no aunts, no sisters. Not one relative came to visit in the sixty-one years, four months, and ten days she lived here. It is what happens when a Japanese woman leaves the family register, released to forever float alone in her decisions.

My mother died before she took off her gardening shoes and turned on the air conditioner. It was a morning routine and included shutting windows and the back door. My brother called to say the coroner decided no autopsy was needed. She was ninety years old and a three-time cancer survivor. She is now high up in her kitchen cabinet. I told my brother his choice is perfect given she couldn't reach high shelves, and she always liked looking down on people. Our mother is in a special transport urn, because my brother thinks ahead. With my sons, we envisioned trekking to Hiroshima next year, driving to a small suburban area, checking into an Airbnb before presenting her ashes to three younger sisters and their adult children. Only they've decided my mother shouldn't return to Japan. There is a legend that when a person leaves the family, they cannot come back. It is bad luck. This is what my mother's sister tells my cousin to Google translate to me. This, from the aunt my mother kept safely hidden in mountain caves while she scavenged for food, picking maggots from yams to keep the family from starving. She and her mother herded the children through those final months before Hiroshima.

My mother said I couldn't ever understand the type of sacrifice needed to survive war. I am not a good Japanese daughter. I don't listen, refuse to let men walk in front of me, laugh too loud, and ask too many questions. She'd be relieved. Her pushy daughter is taking her home regardless of legends, bad luck, or aunts who politely don't want their sister. We'll carry her ashes, a fine powder, a perfect cremation the funeral home said, in a carry-on, tucking it securely into an overhead compartment. We'll transition our words into how Japanese refer to honoring the dead. Cremation is known as bone cutting, and the ceremony is called bone spreading. The Japanese have gotten it right. Our mother's bones are resting after spending a lifetime being cut, fractured, and chipped in preparation for this journey. Returning her to the waters around Hiroshima where she swam as a child, the beaches where she dug her toes into the sand, is what is right for a woman who dreamt of being a teacher, was the fastest runner in her school, whose life was marked by failing to raise an obedient daughter, who survived the terrors of a world war, who forever saw images of the Tokyo fire bombings, Hiroshima, Nagasaki,

bombs,

bombs,

bombs.

My mother came running to a new country, an unblemished place with gold paved roads, no hunger or burned cities, no bullet holes in buildings, no people with the slackened faces of intergenerational trauma, walking with soured mouths repeating shikata ga nai at every disappointment, every insult, and slur thrown by American GI's. She came running, breathless, hopeful, to birth babies on the ground of those who hated her, what she represented, by being a small woman, a nearly five-foot-tall, dark-haired woman, eyes pointed downward, speaking English without pure "r's" or "l's" in broken syllables. Living and dying on stolen ground.

My mother died without finishing her coffee or starting the laundry. She left the back door open, and the heat, the smoke drifted in, and moved around the house. Realizing no one was home, except for a spirit waiting to run free, they carried her outside, high into the ash-filled skies over California.

Justice

by AMANDA L. ANDREI

A liminal space shifting from Hecuba's LA Filipinotown bakery to her memory and dreams.

Violet light.

HECUBA

All of my lovers, I named Priam. I don't remember any of their given names, they are all Priam to me. Men have so many faults, it's best to collapse all those lovers into one man, one ideal, and hope that their faults will cancel each other out and only the good memories will remain.

Of course, you could go the other way, remembering only their faults and none of their good qualities.

I remember one Priam, who kissed me on the hand as he left my house, only a few minutes late after martial law curfew. I never saw him again.

I remember one Priam, who climbed the top of a coconut tree when I was thirteen, just to bring me a green coconut with the freshest juice.

I remember one Priam, so dark he was almost blue, with an accent I had never heard before, who then left on a ship a week later.

I remember one Priam, who worked with me in the newspaper office, who laughed every time I edited his articles, but made the corrections anyway.

I remember one Priam, so kind when I first arrived to this country, who didn't even touch me during our sham marriage, and quietly divorced me with my new citizenship intact.

I remember one Priam, pale and freckled, who thought I was crazy and still loved me for it. I wish he had rejected me instead.

I would tell my unborn daughters, your fathers are all one father – one Priam, a king among men, and you are princesses, each of you – not because your father is a king, but because I am a Queen, and I am so much of a Queen that even when battered and pulled apart by the spirits of war and fury, I can give up my crown and still be royal.

A knock on the door.

HECUBA (CONT'D)

There is no justice in this world.

Do you still believe in spring?

by TANYA KO HONG

from *METRO*

Inspired by the students of my Fairfax High Poetry Workshop during pandemic

A lonely bird knocks
on a kitchen window

Is there still a world? Deserted school
playground, buttercup lip gloss, unopened,

cold french fries, uncertain future
Hope like rotten lemon juice

An ambulance siren sings
Red and white glitter against

sidewalks Tonight someone
dies alone A patch of lotus

flowers exude fragrance
Sunrise yellow, tea green, salmon pink

Though some think it dead, its seeds can germinate for thousands
of years

Later the lotus blooms
magnificent in the deepest mud

I pray this poem finds in your darkness,
hands reaching through ghost light

In the remaining space of this postcard
I write, I still believe in love

Game Day

by VK LYNNE

SYNOPSIS

So here we are, the ass-end of May, something like 10 weeks into the COVID-19 Quarantine, and the already brazen sector of AmeriKKKA has become even more emboldened, so after two high-profile and particularly outlandish executions, it all boils over.

CHARACTERS

The Terrorist in the White House.

An Angry, Fed-up, African-American Citizenry.

A League of Appalled Allies.

A Knot of Desperate Opportunists, fresh from the pages of a Victor Hugo novel, lying in wait.

A Team of Tiny Footballers, in their best game day uniforms of MAGA hats and confederate flag togas.

The terrorist in the White House stands before his base like a former high school bully who wanted to lead his varsity team to glory, but never advanced past the position of water carrier. Now, as a bitter and 'roid-raged adult, he coaches PeeWee League on the weekends, where he's convinced his wide-eyed charges that he's a legend who uses his Heisman trophy as a tie rack and screams military-grade motivation into their ignorant, terrified faces before he throws them out on the field to fight for his glory.

GRANNY

Now children, someday... if there is a "someday"... you will read about the 2020 "Race Riots" (history will no doubt brand them with some pithy, generalized, agenda-laden moniker of that sort), and Granny's here to tell you about how they started this very weekend.

> *I know it seems like you know where all this is going, but this is 'Murica, and I'm building a fable here, so consider the preceding "plot development."*

GRANNY (CONT'D)

The protests were inevitable—who could stay silent?—and, at the outset, they were carefully planned and structured with rules and leaders and all the safeguards that the naive idealists thought would prevent what happened next... the most natural thing in the world...

The sun went down.

And when darkness came, the game was on.

Maybe it was the subliminal commands that were carried on the chants. Because when the Angry, Fed-up, African-American Citizenry and League of Appalled Allies yelled, "No Justice, No Peace," the Team of Tiny Footballers heard "Eat the Rich," and of course, our frothing, over-hyped Terrorist in the White House called, "Hike."

CHILDREN

So what happened Granny?

GRANNY

We all dropped the ball, baby. In the end—we all dropped the ball.

Safer at Home

by THEA PUESCHEL

from *THE ABSTRACT ELEPHANT MAGAZINE*

No one ever thinks it will happen to them. Those things you see in the news. The bolt of lightning that strikes a person. The body left charred. The car that drove through a living room and knocked the house off its foundation. The child hit as he crossed the street, leaving behind red streaks of blood where he once stood. It has always happened to someone else. Not to me. Not to my family. We saw the pandemic strike China, then Italy, and spread. I thanked God; it was them and not us. Things like this don't happen to us. Not my family. Every night we'd praise God for his grace.

The pandemic hit America. The President insisted it was a minor issue being played up in the media. It made sense. It affected no one in my family or friend circle. Then the state shut down. Schools closed. Work was furloughed or became work from home. It even happened to my family.

"Safer at home," they said. We listened until we didn't. Masks were uncomfortable. Hugs in our family are considered a basic human need. The five of us would congregate on the porch on the warm evenings of spring. We'd wave at our neighbors as they walked by. Grandma would crochet or knit vibrant scarves, booties, and doilies. Jonas texted his friends with emojis and dreams of high school graduation. Tom and I held hands. I'd sip chardonnay until my cheeks turned pink. He'd knock back his Budweiser until his breath soured. Tina colored on the sidewalk on hands and knees up to the porch with rainbows and blessings. Her little fingers and palms would be colored pastel. We had never spent so much time together as a family. It was nice.

Our neighbor Roger liked to walk his dog in the evenings, always with a spring in his step and a USA windbreaker. He'd always stop for a chat. That night, he was slow and thoughtful.

From the porch, I shouted, "How's Anne?"

"She's good. She's in pain, but she's good," Roger said, as he paused in front of the house with his white Pekingese.

"I heard it's painful. You need anything?"

"Well, it's the COVID. But you know she'll pull through—Nah, we're good."

It was a shame about Anne, but it happened to their family, not mine. Thank God. Thoughts and prayers and all that. We aren't the type of people these things happen to.

Jonas still worked on the front lines as an essential worker. A bagger at Ralphs. It was a simple job that gave him money to spend and the ability to hang out with his friends. His fifteen-hour weeks turned to forty. School was canceled. He could get the hours. He took them. Every day he'd leave with his old N95 mask that became grubbier with each shift and biker gloves he never washed. In the evening, he'd come back exhausted. He'd tell us stories of people being aggressive over toilet paper or other limited supplies.

Grandma snuck off to her bible study group every day when we weren't looking. She'd Uber, or have the pastor come pick her up in his lime green Saturn. Even though the news told her that she should stay at home, being vulnerable and all. She still went.

I'm not sure who developed the first cough. It had to be Grandma or Jonas. Tom worked from home and managed his global team. Tina Zoom schooled third grade. I was laid off from being a contract Imagineer at Disneyland. After years of waiting to be hired. Then the pandemic. Mimosas and Bloody Mary brunches became my self-care. Even in my current buzzed state, I knew it wasn't the three of us.

A month ago, grandma came home in the middle of the

afternoon complaining of body aches and pains, which was nothing new. She was 90. Everything hurt anyway. It wasn't until she was confused and had trouble breathing that we called for an ambulance. She passed on the way to the hospital. We assumed it was old age until we were told to self-quarantine for 14 days by the health department. Her church live-streamed her memorial service. It was beautiful. Even with our intermittent connection.

Jonas was pissed and resistant to stay at home. His teenage angst boiled up into arguments about fairness. Five days later, he struggled to stay awake. He just couldn't do it. I thought it was a growth spurt. His dry cough had worsened and proved otherwise. He was alone in the ICU with beeping monitors. Struggling to breathe. Without access to a ventilator. My sweet boy expired. Alone. This didn't happen to people like us; they said so in the news.

Tina ran a high fever and became listless. I found her eight-year-old body cloaked in sweat. Crumpled on the floor in her fairy princess costume. I scooped her up. Yelled for Tom to get the car. We went to the emergency room. We were separated and told to go home. They carried our limp little girl away. The ER nurses were kind and let us Facetime our little one. She was scared and confused. They streamed her last breaths for us. Thankfully, the connection remained stable. Unlike my emotional state. I don't know how this happened to us. We weren't people things happened to. Once probable, but highly unlikely. Definitely not twice. Thrice didn't even seem possible. I heard it's called cognitive dissonance.

From there, it's a blur. Tom's death didn't even register. I knew he was gone because there was plenty of Bud in the refrigerator. I just don't remember when.

The news didn't tell me how I should feel. It was inconsistent. It was a political plague; they said. I expected it to come for grandma as flues often take the old. The rest took me by surprise. Healthy and young. That was supposed to make them invulnerable. Now I am stuck in a looping stage of grief. I fluctuate between the numbness of denial and the heaviness of despair. I'm on the brink of acceptance. There were five of us. Now I'm the only one. It happened to us. Not to me—just my family. Each. One. Gone. Hugs and coughs were the death of us. That, and a fractured nation.

Color Blind

by TRICIA PARK

The sky is blue. But everyone around me insists that the sky is red.

What if your whole life, you were told, "The sky is red, the sky is red, the sky is red, the sky is red"? After a lifetime of being force fed this lie, wouldn't you believe, then, that the sky *is* red or, at the very least, wouldn't you learn to repress your own belief?

Even if you *know* that the sky is blue.

Because every time you've been asked: "What color is the sky?" or worse yet, "What color do *you* think the sky is?" maybe you've answered, tentatively, "Well, you know, I'm not sure but I think it might be blue." Or maybe you've been defiant, maybe you've somehow found the courage to yell, "It's *blue*, goddammit, it's *blue*!"

And every time you've tried to tell people that you can *see* that the sky is blue and that you *know* that they've been gaslighting you, then:

They berate you, scolding you, like a child: "No! I told you a million times, the sky is red!"

Or they humiliate you: "What're you, stupid? The sky is red, everyone knows that. What is *wrong* with you?"

Or they negate you, patronizing you: "No, uh-uh, no way, the sky is red, no one thinks the sky is blue. You're imagining things."

Or they confront you with their own wounded feelings: "How could you say that to me? I mean, is there something *I* did to make you think the sky is blue?"

Or they accuse you of hypersensitivity: "No one is forcing you to think the sky is blue. If *you* want to think that the sky is blue, you can think that but that's on *you*, because you take everything *way* too personally. No one's making you think the sky is blue."

Or they shame you, triangulate you against other groups: "I mean, that's not really that bad is it? You only *think* the sky is blue while those other folks over there, they're *surrounded* by blueness."

Or they think you should take it as a compliment, fetishizing you: "Tell me about the 'blue' sky. I'm fascinated by your Blueness, I think it's so exotic and beautiful. I want to experience your Blueness."

When the light finally finds us, being in the spotlight is threatening. After being ignored, bullied, erased, for years and years and years, all of a sudden, the attention of the dominant culture—White consciousness—is peering down at you. And you're expected to perform. And it better be good—perfect, actually—because who knows when you'll get another chance.

Now, all of a sudden, because traumatic and heinous things are visible, everyone wants to know what you think about the color of the sky. And they're asking you to teach them about how they, too, might see the sky as blue.

But the thing is, you've spent a lifetime unlearning everything about the sky's blueness, repressing your thoughts and feelings to change the very patterns of your brain.

What if you're only just learning how to identify—let alone process, label, and explain to others—what it is you've been experiencing? What if you're ontologically challenged, existentially confused, because you're so practiced at doubting your own experiences and feelings and thoughts? What if you've been gastlit for so long that you've learned to invert everything, like a film negative. Because in the absence of inclusion, our need to belong is so intense and essential that we will shapeshift in order to fit the tribe, even if this means we vanish and reject ourselves.

I've spent a whole life redwashing the blueness.

And now, the redseers are still trying to explain to me that this is not really about seeing blue but about something else, something conveniently less heinous, something like one individual's perversion. And how he shot all those women who look like me because he was having a "really bad day."

One "bad apple's" "bad day."

Because after all, the criminals—these monsters—are redseers. So they don't want this one redseer to represent all redseers. The redseers are very anxious that we all understand that. You see, they're not like that *one* redseer. Whereas if it had been a blueseer that had done this heinous despicable thing, well the answer would be—always is—it's because they see the sky as blue. The blueseers always, always, always represent *all* blueseers because that is the only thing that is notable about the blueseers: their inability to see the sky as red. This fundamental flaw reduces all of us blueseers to our blueness; redseers are the righteous, moral, correct side of things so if any one redseer does something horrific, well, they're the exception to the rule. The blueseer, on the other hand, is always *proof* of the rule; therefore, blueseers, you better not ever, ever, ever fall out of line.

Blueseers have to be perfect and even then, it's never enough.

So, if seeing the sky as blue is a fundamental flaw, what makes you think I'm ever going to admit that I see the sky as blue, let alone talk about it.

"But no, no, we see that the sky is blue," the redseers admit, and in fact, some of them whisper it to me, like I'm their fucking confessor, "in fact, we always kind of knew that the sky was blue.

We just didn't want you to know that we knew."

Or some of them will be shocked and weep at my feet, "Oh my god, we're so sorry that we didn't realize the sky was blue and we feel so *bad* about it. Please, please, please teach me how to see the blue sky. I want to learn and be a blue sky *ally.*"

And now you want me to explain all of it to you. And I better do it quick and perfectly because *hurry up hurry up* who knows how long we'll have this moment, who knows how long before the flood lights shut off and the spotlight burns out or, more likely, some more brilliant, incandescent, sensational blueness will flare up bright in another corner, on another stage, while the redseers sit back in their seats, inhaling popcorn as they gape, critiquing all of our performances. Deciding whether they think my account, my telling, my performance of my own blue experience is compelling enough. Is my blueness, violent, tragic, tear-jerking enough?

It's still the redseer that decides whether it "counts."

All of us blueseers have been pressed up against the doors of a megastore called the "American Dream", aka equality, opportunity, meritocracy, fairness. A lie. A place where all the redseers live inside and drink hot cocoa and fine wine while we wait on line for millenia, the queue extending in front and behind into infinity, our fingers frostbitten, our skin scorched as the seasons rotate in an unending cycle, and after centuries of waiting, the megastore door suddenly bursts open. We're discombobulated and then we scramble, because who knows when this moment might happen—or not happen—again. "Speak up, speak up, now is the moment!" Voices shout and echo, desperate: "This is your chance! Speak up!"

But what if I'm not ready.

Or I will speak up, or I *am* speaking up, I just don't want to be crushed in the mob.

Or I'm too exhausted from waiting, to rush into the megastore and grab my share.

And if I burn everything down, what then?
Will the mob turn on me?
Does this make me a traitor?
Does this make me complicit?

There is grief in the realization that we were *right* all along: that the sky *is* blue. The redseers have always known this, oppressing me and all blueseerers, for generations.

What if it's also unclear if everyone will ever truly agree on the color of the sky?

And what if the sky changes?

The Stories We Tell Ourselves: The Power of Narrative and Community Amid Chaos

by KATE MARUYAMA

from *ENTROPY MAGAZINE*

I am still trying to make sense of the summer of 2017 when my mother lost her mind and the country seemed to lose its. And the stories we told ourselves to find our way through.

"I think everyone's really sad and feeling weird because of Trump. Like everyone I talk to is weird." My mom sounded worried, afraid. Not like herself.

I said, "Describe weird." Her description was paranoid, dark, apocalyptic. Something was off.

When I had to convince her that the dear friend she said she was having lunch with the following week had died a year before, I knew something bigger was wrong. I begged her not to drive anymore and placed a deluge of phone calls to friends, doctors, the insurance company, and by remote, set up appointments which led to the MRI that sent my whole world sideways. Mom, the narrative center of my life, the holder of all the family and literary stories had glioblastoma, evidenced by a tumor the size of a walnut growing in her corpus callosum.

We had assembled in Skira Martinez's Cielo Galleries, a live/work space in South Central Los Angeles. A motley handful of us sat on sofas in a sunny white room noshing on snacks with Chiwan Choi and Peter Woods while their Writ Large partner Judeth Oden Choi managed a vast graph documenting 90 days, starting in July, that were to be filled with cultural events as Writ Large Press entered its second iteration of 90x90LA. Representatives from different L.A. communities spitballed, planning a consortium on disability, conversations around gentrification, cultural erasure, immigration, as well as readings, writing workshops for kids, nights of music, and poems.

It was to be called *90x90LA: Resist.* Marching, writing letters, making phone calls weren't enough. Trump had galvanized and mobilized racial hatred, ableism, sexism, homophobia. He had made the country dangerous for anyone not a cisgender hetero white male. This response of creating safe spaces for folks not in that category was something I wanted to be a part of. It was movement and creativity during a time we felt paralyzed.

In most people's personal narratives, my mom was loud and vibrant. She was a constant, energetic supporter of her friends and the literary community—putting people together was her specialty. "Oh, you should really know each other." This was the truth whenever she said it, and countless publications, partnerships, or new creative pieces always emerged from these meetings.

She was a fierce advocate for anyone marginalized within the literary or academic communities in which she lived. She had come up in the 1950s in all-male newsrooms and recognized folks who had to hustle more and fight harder to be heard, let alone get work. She was always ready online or in person with a meal, support, or advice. And she was always, always, at the other end of the phone any time I had a question, problem, or funny story to share.

And then she wasn't.

We moved her out to LA for treatment. She was supposed to do readings for her book tour. So swiftly did this tumor change her that when she finally arrived, I had to do that first reading for her, with her sitting next to me. By the second reading a week later she was delusional, so I left her home with my family and read for her. I had to say something to the crowd about her absence that wouldn't make me fall to pieces at the microphone. I think I said she was "under the weather."

This joyful celebration of a new book rapidly morphed into a frantic dance around the knowledge that it was her last book, as her cognitive mechanics misfired and finally ran down.

By the time 90x90LA began in July, the logistics and medical paperwork around my parents had become dizzying as I dealt with my regular life as well; my teenagers wrapped up their school year, and I closed out my writing workshops from spring. In the meantime, we had moved my dad, whom Alzheimer's had put in a wheelchair, out to Los Angeles as well. We set him up in the same care facility as my mom, and for his move-in interview, a few questions from the staff revealed that Dad was now the more together parent of the two. Mom had all of Dad's stories. Now everyone was gone.

Despite everything, I kept 90x90LA on the schedule. These were spaces where words, prose, poetry, and conversation were aired, music was playing, and people of color, women, non-binary folk, Muslim folk, people with disabilities—people from so many different groups attacked daily by a new president—felt safe to speak and express strength and rage, and their knowledge that this country that had never protected them had them lashing out in a more aggressive way. The narrative that 90x90LA pushed forward was: no matter what, people need safe community spaces.

One Thursday a month, Peter Woods from Writ Large ran Read Beats at the LA Theater Company during LA's Art Walk; a perfect example about how different organizations working together form community. The Drunken Masters Series brought out masters in a genre: poetry, fiction, songwriting and liquored them up so they could offer hilarious, but always kind, feedback to new artists. On Wednesdays Traci Akemi Kato-Kiriyama ran a Wellness Writing workshop, where in the quiet of the Aratani Theater in Little Tokyo people gathered for writing exercises and conversation. Workshops were offered on grant-writing, there were gatherings for Korean adoptees to share their experiences, and Soul Together provided a safe space for POC to gather and support and share. Every event I attended sent me home filled with gratitude for friends, inspiring words, new ways of looking at things, and the energy to go on.

We were told by doctors that my mother's type of tumor reacts well to radiation. It was 60% possible that they'd shrink the tumor and she'd come back to us mentally and we could say goodbye properly. She would know that we loved her. It was hard to tell what she knew at this point, as she was no longer speaking. She was a writer who had lost her thread. I was left to narrate what I thought her needs were, at that moment.

I had dropped the out-and-about L.A. field trips I usually took with my kids in the summers, due to everyday radiation appointments I split with my brother. They took four hours: driving to and from Duarte, getting Mom into a wheelchair, getting her checked into radiation, making a bathroom pitstop, changing Mom's diaper, getting lunch, feeding her lunch, getting her back into the car, back to her facility. By the time I returned home, I had nothing left to give, to feel, to think with. I was an empty, black shell and curled up with my daughter on my bed where we watched TV. We chose plotlines that did not contain cancer, fear, or despair.

Curled up in front of an episode of *Separated at Birth,* my daughter asked me a question I didn't hear. I asked her to repeat it and she fell silent. She had tears in her eyes. She asked, "Is brain cancer contagious?" She was certain I had caught it. I had lost my mother and she was losing hers.

Traci Akemi Kato-Kiriyama set up The Cultural Spine for 90x90LA so that people could "take their shoes off," come into Little Tokyo and learn about its history. That evening it was so nice to see faces I knew, to finally get my kids out of the house walking around on a golden summer evening in downtown L.A., the buildings glowing in red brick, the sky a saturated blue.

I pushed back the black cloud of my mother's illness and learned from Traci, Scott Oshima from Sustainable Little Tokyo, and L.A. historian and poet Mike Sonksen how the Japanese community had been on First Street in Little Tokyo for over a hundred years. Despite mass deportation, incarceration, and gentrification, this city's every trick toward erasure, the community pushed back. People pooled money and resources to protect each other with jobs and housing, promoting local pride and reclaiming space where they could. While eating mochi, we learned that the owners of Fugetsudo, where it was made, buried their equipment in the basement when they were incarcerated in concentration camps during World War II. Now their business is among the longest running in L.A. at 100 years. We learned about resilience, and this summer it was something we sorely needed to hear. It wasn't a narrative of hope exactly, but proof that hanging on might just be a way to get through. That there might be an *after.* If we could reframe this summer from apocalyptic to temporary, maybe that would be something.

The story of Los Angeles I had learned before I moved here was: There was *nothing but farmland* and a few white folks came out and created the amazing and all-consuming film industry, which had in turn created the "sprawling" metropolis it is today. In my twenty-five years here, that narrative has been proven a complete falsehood. Here we were, feet to the ground in Little Tokyo, in a clear, location-specific hundred-year-long narrative. I thought how deeply false and dangerous the white story of Los Angeles was, and I knew white people in the city who still subscribed to it. I knew now that early Los Angeles was a thriving agricultural city where Japanese, Chinese and Mexican people, as well as freemen, worked in each other's businesses and on each other's land; how the city, the farms, the businesses were comfortably multicultural at the turn of the 19th to 20th century. I knew how a few white people started coming out after oil and gold, and how they flooded the city to find a place in the film industry. Racist housing practices only started in the 1920s when there were enough white people to start declaring what was theirs. They co-opted Chinatown. They took land from Little Tokyo. The Cultural Spine tour filled in an important part of this history.

Traci always reminded us that we were standing on Tongva land, that erasure began centuries before. Knowing the complicated nature of our history, good and bad, is the only way to avoid repeating it.

The black cloud hadn't gone, my mother's illness was real. Still, I was buoyed, near elated by this tour. And, feet to the ground, my kids were connecting with their city and its history.

My mom's greatest skill was that, reporter-trained, she asked questions and listened. Her life wove through those around her in a way she never bragged about. If asked about these deeds she'd shrug and say, "It's just what you do."

She could not at this point turn her head.

Her friends sent her emails as if she were really there. *You'll be happy to hear,* and *I know you'll find this hilarious* or *you probably already know, but I was surprised to learn.* There were also so many *Get well soon. Keep fighting.* I sent hopeful emails back, *We are going to radiation, we are fighting cancer, we are hoping.*

As a human race, we have always told ourselves stories to stay afloat, to get through. I realize even here, that is what I'm doing. Shaping a narrative.

Poet, artist and activist Tanzila Ahmed had put together a reading for Ramadan. We sat in the gallery space of Skira's Cielo Galleries in chairs surrounded by a beautifully lit installation of sculptures of women's torsos, each painted in a different style. The gallery served its local community in South Central. It was important to Writ Large that their events incorporate community and Cielo Galleries was a living, breathing part of its South Central community.

Before the reading began, I sat in the darkened gallery, the painted torsos glowing in their key lights along the walls. I was talking with my friends, Art and Rocío, both poets. For the first time aloud, I said, "My mother is dying." It felt like pressure escaping a can, it had been let out into this space, and made me quiet enough to listen.

The Muslim community was reeling from the Muslim Ban and the dangerous, rabble-rousing toxicity of our new president. Thirty to forty people from different communities had shown up to this space to hear these poems. Each poem was a journey. They were stunning, sad, fierce, beautiful, and sometimes hilarious. They were all real and carried the listener into the poet's experience of being Muslim in an anti-Muslim country. I thought of Little Tokyo's trauma from mass incarceration in WWII and this new and present reality, where the fear of that sort of mass transport, attempted erasure was very real. There was a great deal for us to process from the news every day, all of it outrageous, incendiary. But in these smaller spaces and dark rooms was clarity amidst the binary argumentative narratives of the daily media. How could we stop all of this mounting hate and tribalism in this country?

And what is losing one parent, an aged parent, against everything going on?

My kids' grandmother was dying, but, thanks to 90x90LA they were finally learning what it was to be citizens of their city.

I took my son down to the meeting on gentrification, again, in Skira's space. We sat in a sunlit bright white circle in the gallery full of people from various neighborhoods all over Los Angeles. We listened as people from dozens of different communities spoke of rising rents, displaced elders, and powerlessness in the face of a city that did not care about erasure, displacement; that did not seem to care about its residents. It was a local echo of what was going on nationally. This fit into the Little Tokyo narrative so well. This history was not new to the city, it had been going on since white people had arrived, and before that, when the Tongva were first displaced.

Because I could not say my mom was dying every time I spoke to someone, the story of everything that had happened since May became small. "I moved my parents out here to live with us," was met with a, "how nice." I stopped talking to most but the closest of friends and that was usually by email. I didn't want to hear my voice crack.

Radiation finished and the doctor told us "The tumor has outgrown the treatment." Her oncologist said we didn't need to bring her anymore. That daily battle to get her body from wheelchair to car to wheelchair had ended. I was helpless with the idea that maybe it didn't have to have happened in the first place.

We were sent to hospice and were told we had only a week or two. Mom, determined as ever, ended up sticking around for five weeks. Hell no, she wouldn't go.

I thought of the family stories that disappeared with my father's Alzheimer's that I was no longer able to triangulate with my mother. This loss of narrative is its own grief.

Thursday mornings became about going to Little Tokyo for PUBLISH!, the name of the first event Writ Large ever held and the most specific example of the good work they do. The idea is to get folks to write, wherever they are, wherever it's set up (Union Station, metro stops, book fairs), going back to the root of the word *publish*, meaning making words "public." This iteration of PUBLISH! was a space created under tents in the middle of the broad, red-bricked JACCC plaza in Little Tokyo. For three weeks running on Thursday mornings there was a prompt, "What was home then? What is home now?" written out in English, Japanese, and Spanish in the hopes of capturing stories of those who had lived through incarceration, through the damage to pursuant generations in Little Tokyo. Every Thursday, Traci, Chiwan, Rocío and I showed up.

But the people didn't. When we wrapped the last day and turnout was not what we expected, rather than deeming the event a failure, Traci said, "This is good." People *not* showing up became its own talking point to open new channels of communication for the various groups in little Tokyo; it had given her a new entry into opening up organization within the community. Something as simple as changing the narrative from, "This didn't work," to "This is good," was a lesson in grace in narrative. And I needed this grace now on a personal and national level. This summer would not stop teaching me how the way in which we shape our stories is sometimes more important than what actually happens.

My mother died three nights later, September 24th.

When the dust has settled and we have moved on to this country's next iteration, I hope the memories will be like this. That we came through a dark time, but we were surrounded by people who cared and worked together to push back, who reached out of their own circles to take care of each other. And that, along the way, people found the power of changing their own place in the national story.

Instead of decrying the failures, I hope that we can look at the change, find the opportunities and say, "This is good" and move forward. That we can flip the narrative toward hope and action.

My mother's fingerprints are all over two generations of family, and a legion of friends made better for her having been here. I'm so lucky for the time I had with her. I'm having trouble going on without her. These things are both true.

I keep writing, hoping to make sense of this story. I keep looking around me to find ways to help. That's all I can do for now.

Cut Fruit and Castella

by JULES CHUNG

from *THE LUMIERE REVIEW*

crammed into the main room of the apartment
grandmother, aunts and uncles, cousins, sisters,
one brother, shy because he's outnumbered
and forlorn away from his console,
we press in gracefully, no one crowds

even in skirts we sit on gleaming yellow floors
like nobles, legs turned just so, like fine furnishings,
the pale sofas remain immaculate
through several rounds of fruit and cake

the pears, the melon, the peaches, the castella
the fruit cut like gems, ripe and perfect as legend
the cake pillowy and gold, boldly subtle, un-iced
the conversation and laughter in Korean
fluid between the elders, flowing between the young
as we use hands, faces, and broken off chunks
of language to cross over and understand

my mother's family is warm and welcoming
reuniting means flying and driving forever
once a decade if they're lucky
there's only time for sweetness

so clean the knife and slice more fruit
wipe it clean and cut more cake

Cardamom Vowels

by ARUNI WIJESINGHE

from *ANGELS FLIGHT LITERARY WEST*

Your name is not
an apology, the sound kowtowing
to ears accustomed to Jennifers
and Debbies. You are a namesake
for a temple rising
in the Chao Phraya River,
face to the morning sun. Your name
is mantra, meant for repetition.

Your name is not
a question, voice rising at the end.
Unlearn the habit
of asking. Hold the magic
of Sanskrit in your throat.
Orient yourself with definitions:
red dawns, lotus offerings,
the padding steps of lions' feet
in forests of rare trees,
groves that tremble incantation.

Your name is not
a punchline. You are not obliged
to accept awkward nicknames
and laugh, not required
to contort your tongue
into a foreign shape. Don't grow towards
mispronunciation, dividing yourself
into two people. Remove ill-fitting shoes
that chafe along the seams; roam
barefoot in the halls of your name.

Unlearn a lifetime
of answering to
not your name. Make them taste
your name, their unknowing tongues
prickling with tamarind.
Shape their mouths around
cardamom vowels,
your syllables turmeric. Teach them
to whisper spice, intone fire.

Grab and Go

by CECILIA CABALLERO

from *RAISING MOTHERS*

They give us food here.
My mother always taught me to look
Inside the clearance bin at grocery stores
All the way in the back back, the bar code
Sliced through with a permanent marker
And a new handwritten price, fifty cents or a dollar.
Here, they place the food on plastic picnic tables
Here, they give us almost expired chocolates on Fridays
One day there were golden balloons tied to a tall parking cone
A celebration of sorts, if you squint a little at all the food
One day, I took a frozen tray and bit into a cheese ravioli
Before I noticed a dark mass multiplying like a tumor
Across my fork and down my throat from the bits I already ate.
I spat it out.
And went back for more the next day.

I wear a mask the color of my mother's hair.
That I bought at Smart & Final around the corner
Did you know there is a national coin shortage?
I saw a sign there at the register. What do the
People living at the park do now?
An economy that saves lives with the currency of coins.

An abuelita in front of me pushes an empty baby stroller for
    her food
A viejito holds a dandelion yellow bag from Forever 21
We push and pull our food back to our familias
A jacaranda petal falls into a curl of my hair, inside my bag,
    the cement.

The trees are not surprised to see this sickness
They observe how we gather food now.
I walk and a man inside a truck
Who looks like my father
Slows down, leans over, demands, “Donde vas?”
I grab and go. A prayer for protection.
My mother taught me this too.
A desperation that usually doesn’t work.
The trees know this too.

My mask cannot deter men
Like that man in the truck, like my father,
And probably your father too.
My mask, my sweater, my food for my child
The man’s breath and his threat is noxious in the air
See how it binds with the smog from the freeway
Lifetimes of soot within my lungs, the bronchioles,
Pulmonary veins, the diaphragm a container for both lungs
 and grief.

At home, I close the door to the world and we feast
On little pouches of cold baby carrots, fresh apples,
Hamburgers with too much gristle and grease, cheese pizza
Smeared with thick hydrogenated oils that the tongue
Cannot wick away from the mouth, cookies and cakes,
And rotten raviolis.

These become parts of my son’s new cells
The lining of his tissues, the marrow of his bones
Producing platelets and pleas to live another day.
Because a brown boy almost his age was shot in the back a few
 years ago.
Just down the street. A police officer did it. He is alive. The boy
 is not.
But they don’t know that my son’s blood produces pandemics
 too.

Can you hear it? When the bones release blood? It is like a boiling.
The next day, I am on the sidewalk again
Lined with purple petals of possibilities.
The jacaranda taught me this.

Parchita / Passion Poetry

by LISBETH COIMAN

To all those forever condemned to a life of tasteless fruits
Apples that can only adorn a pig's mouth
or be thrown at a doctor's head
Needy of spices for a semblance of flavor in a pie
Pears unworthy of my taste buds
unless bathed in hot syrup with the aromatic clove in it
Strawberries seasoned with the sweat of
undocumented labor in California's fields

To those who have never enjoyed the heat of the tropics
I offer my hand
pregnant with the perfume of
a tropical vine growing wild in my homeland
Parchita, daffodil-yellow and oval   the size of a duck's egg
withered in appearance when ripe

Cut in two   it releases a
a cornucopia of flavors   citrusy and tart
Scoop a teaspoonful of its
slimy bright orange pulp   entangled
    with abundant black seeds
Pour aged rum   distilled burnt sugar
into the Sweet Cup   will make a sibar of you
Blended and drained the Granadilla juice will refresh
    a worker in a hot afternoon
Add it to cream to make the most exquisite of desserts
    Mousse de Parchita
a longing that haunts my dreams
bittersweet   like a lover saying goodbye after a night of
    vibrant sex
creamy yellow in the center soft   like clouds in September

Take it between your hands   bring it to your lips
Be delighted with the way it tantalizes your taste buds

the explosion of colors sparking in your mouth
Caribbean Sea
canopy of the jungle in Canaima
snow of the Andes
pasture of Los Llanos
soil of Barlovento
south slope of El Avila in April
sun over my head at high noon

Drink from its shell
A supernova of aromas will wrap itself around your hands
    your mouth
even your breast where it will drop its desirable viscosity
intoxicating   like the smell of cocoa beans freshly harvested
reassuring   like the scent of coffee at four am
earthy moist cloud rising from the hot soil of the gardens after
    a sudden shower in May
interrupting the afternoon impromptu baseball games in
    the neighborhood
iodized salty foam of the waves softly eroding the sandcastles
    of my childhood
essence of the homeland I can't return to

García Marquez's guava got nothing on the smell of my parchita

Take my hand so the curly sprouts of the exuberant passiflora
    lilikoi
wondrous flower   can lace themself around your fingers
until you   too   can offer the fragrance of this
    magnificent creation
to all those forever condemned to a life of tasteless fruits

A circle of women may just be the most powerful force known to humanity. If you have one, embrace it. If you need one, seek it. If you find one, for the love of all that is good and holy, dive in. Hold on. Love it up. Get Naked. Let them see you. Let them hold you. Let your reluctant tears fall. Let yourself rise fierce and love gentle. You will be changed. The very fabric of your being will be altered by this, if you allow it.

Jeanette LeBlanc

Ode to Samarasa Center

by ALEXANDRA SHECKLER

It was more than a yoga studio. It was the daily commitment. The front door catching mid-swing. The immediacy of incense. The collective *Hi, Alexandra.* Removing my shoes, sliding them under the bench. Exhaling after a long day like *Honey, I'm home.* A safe space when everything felt like too much. Palo santo and tea lights as ritual. Matching the color of yoga mat to mood. The click of 'assist' chips on the floor—always 'assist.' Her mat next to mine. One hour in a room with friends, strangers, community. Those damn gorgeous murals. *This wall is also awareness* written in pencil. Bodies full of light. The breath of it.

Coming out of Savasana, that halfway between. Her voice like a smile, breaking the silence. Hugging honey-slow legs. The burning of sweetgrass. Offering our highest selves for the benefit of all beings. The sound of bare feet on wooden floor. Folding my blanket Kripalu style. Marking the challenge chart with stickers. Steeping herbal tea. Staying after to talk and then saying, *Goodnight, lovely people*, with naïve certainty that I could do it all over again tomorrow, and the next day, and the next. Spotting the moon from Sunset Boulevard. Calling my mom to say, *I just got out of class.*

Gathering has taken on a different shape since Samarasa Center shuttered its doors during the pandemic. Remaining members now practice together online. Seeing these faces, hearing these voices, being in this community still feels to me like sanctuary; home.

A Nun and a Pop Star: How They Helped Me Through the Pandemic

by LAURA STURZA

from MEDIUM'S *P.S. I LOVE YOU*

In our past year's stay-at-home lifestyle, my familiar foundations were shaken loose, my experience of time and space radically altered, and the daily mix of anxiety, grief and tenderness made me yearn to reconnect with far-flung friends from different eras of my life, blurring the lines between past and present.

In the uncertain days of the pandemic, I found an unlikely pair of spiritual guides to help me through it: American Buddhist nun Pema Chödrön and Madonna. Since the lockdown began, the words of these two completely different, but very powerful personalities—a nun and a pop star—coaxed me into a more expansive frame of mind. It helped ease isolation and provided the ability to exist in two places at once—my current home in Rockville, Maryland, and my former hometown, Los Angeles.

In 2017, my husband and I moved from L.A. to Maryland to help care for my mother, who needed some extra help. Doing so was a great decision. But three years later, the potent forces that attract wannabee stars to L.A. still pull me back. The city, with its extraordinary mash-up of architectural designs, relentless sun and indie movies at Laemmle Theaters, held an allure that kept me there for 20 years. But if my sadness over leaving the West Coast was only about cultural and natural attractions, D.C. can go head-to-head with L.A. For example, by leaving drought-ridden L.A. I was ecstatic when I got drenched in my first East Coast rainstorm, even though I had just seen my fabulous new D.C.

hairdresser. And before the lockdown started, I could add the free museums, the fragility of cherry blossoms, and Rock Creek Park to the D.C. region's calling cards.

Those lifestyle elements matter, but it was the people I left behind in Southern California that caused me heartbreak. Since our move, we had taken semi-annual trips back to L.A. But when we all became stay-at-home people, I had to find another way to visit; and here is where the nun and the pop star come in.

Pema Chödrön outlines the practice of loving-kindness in her book *The Places That Scare You, A Guide to Fearlessness in Difficult Times*. "We begin by engendering loving-kindness for ourselves and then expand it at our own pace to include loved ones, friends, 'neutral' persons, those who irritate us, all of the above as a group, and finally, all beings through time and space."

I realized I could embrace Chödrön's concept of loving-kindness by experiencing myself with everyone I care about at once—equally with those in California and Maryland. And expanding further, I could tap into my connection to people around the world, human beings on every continent facing the same fears, uncertainties, and moments of grace that I am.

But just as I have found respite in Chödrön's philosophy, I have also turned to a more earthly source to facilitate my spiritual cross-country travels—Madonna's song, *Hollywood*. Ever since I moved back east, this bouncy tune captivated me, connecting with my former West Coast life by dancing along to it. But since adjusting to our new, distanced way of life, Madonna's song took on a deeper meaning for me. I walked in Maryland on one blissfully sunny, spring afternoon, playing it over and over.

There's something in the air in Hollywood
The sun is shining like you knew it would
You're riding in your car in Hollywood
You got the top down and it feels so good

Listening to it, I realized it made me feel like I was as much in Hollywood as in Rockville. And while I'm extremely pleased that we moved closer to Mom, I have come to realize I might never fall out of love with L.A. Because, while it's easy enough for me to feel at home in either city, I am now 2,700 miles from people with whom I'd forged deep friendships for two decades.

But for more than a year, none of us could socialize outside of our homes. We all had to find new ways to be close, no matter where we live. Like me, many of my friends have family members providing essential services in hospitals and elsewhere on the front lines. Together, we have held our breath hoping those we love had the immunity they needed to sustain themselves. I continue holding each of these people close in my heart, writing love notes, staying tethered.

In spite of it all, even while we stayed in our homes, and in between crying jags about the devastation the pandemic has caused, I am determined to welcome moments of joy. I have found that our hearts can connect in ways that make time and distance less relevant. And in our beautifully intertwined world, I can picture Pema Chödrön and Madonna on a Zoom meeting, laying down beats for their first single together. I can hardly wait for it to drop.

Resolution

by DEBORAH EDLER BROWN

from *IMMIGRANT STATUS, A CHAPBOOK OF THE LOS ANGELES NATIONAL POETRY SLAM TEAM*

This summer
I will give up being mean to my finger,
blaming it   for not being male,
                        for not having lips,
blaming it   for being my only inheritance.

This summer
my finger and I will make peace.
It will, after all, be with me longer
than any penis will be.
And I will abandon it
as soon as warm eyes look my way,
and it will pick up books and write,
do dishes and tie shoes until I need it again,
and there it will be – faithful, never far.

This summer
I am making peace with solitude.
Even in a crowd, solitude grabs you.
Even in a marriage. It sneaks up
and bites you on the back of the neck,
pulls you into unexpected embrace.
You can fight it,
or you can surrender,
but there you are anyway,
half naked on the kitchen floor,
wrapped and tangled in solitude.

This summer
I am sowing seeds of sorrow.
You can't escape sorrow,
so I'd rather grow my own.

Then I can vouch for its potency,
know how high the bread will rise,
what kind of jam will sweeten small bites.

This summer
I am sitting on the front porch
with my finger and my solitude,
munching sorrow with strawberry jam.

You are welcome to join me.
I will happily trade my finger for yours,
happily spread jam wherever you like,
but there are crumbs in my bed,
and solitude lurks in the closet.
You can hang yours there.
We can nibble sorrow off each other.
Maybe, between us, we can find a new crop
for the rows in between.

This summer
I will be on my porch waiting.
The rocker is sturdy.
I'm not patient, but I am stubborn.
That saves me.

Come see me this summer.
Bring your penis and your solitude.
My finger and I will be here until fall.
Then I may pack up a few loaves,
head down a new road,
my finger with me, of course.

We Are All Strangers

by SUZANNE C. MARTINEZ

from *BULL & CROSS*

I love the first day of class each year. The oil paint and turpentine aromas become concentrated in August, when they close the building for the summer. I inhale its heady perfume as I click-clack across the painted wood floor in my mules, wearing my street clothes. Everything in the drawing studio at the art college is freshly painted white or pale gray for classes resuming in September, except the wooden easels. The morning light streams in the southeast-facing, floor-to-ceiling windows at an angle that diffuses some of the harshness. I'll observe it travel across the length of the studio and disappear during the four-hour class. Usually, no one takes notice of me until I open the small door leading to my cubicle and close it behind me. They're all scoping each other out like a mob of meerkats on the savanna.

I've been modeling for Donahue's drawing class and painting workshops at the art school on and off for more than twenty-five years, so I've worked out a little routine I follow every time. To begin with, I wear very loose clothing especially undergarments to avoid any pressure lines on my legs, back, or ankles. They're very distracting when someone is drawing the figure. As I've aged, I realize this is very important. And I arrive at least fifteen minutes before class to allow myself time to disrobe and read a few pages of my current book before I pose. I need something to think about while I'm up on the stand.

It's sort of a funny story how I got into modeling back in the seventies. My gorgeous older sister was asked to pose for a sculpture class. The post-war students were complaining about the plaster casts they'd been using to learn to draw the human form for a hundred years. The GI Bill guys wanted real, breathing flesh. They earned it, right? She did it for the cash money it paid and the flexible hours. And because of her husband who'd returned from Viet Nam suffering from stuff he couldn't control, except her. He monitored her like she was a fugitive in witness protection, refused to let her work or give her any money of her own. They had no kids, and she was bored silly hanging around their one-bedroom apartment dusting the same lamp everyday. Modeling was quick money and hers alone. Anyway, she fell in love with the instructor, divorced her husband, and they moved to Paris. I needed a second job, so I took over for her, but no one's asked me to go anywhere yet.

When I'm not modeling, I play the cello, my first love. As wonderful as it would have been to land a permanent gig in a symphony orchestra or in musical theater, it's never happened. I've auditioned hundreds of times, but never get the nod. A few of us from the conservatory started playing together thirty years ago and they eventually became my family. Our string quartet plays at two masses every Sunday at St. Hedwig's plus rehearsals on Tuesday nights, as well as the odd wedding or funeral. And I work as a soloist at a bar mitzvah every so often. I keep my weekday job at the art school my little secret. I'm afraid Father Keenan might be scandalized, titillated, or both.

I peek out of my little door and watch the new crop of kids stroll in alone or in groups of two or three. They look like such babies; it's hard to believe they're college students. Over the years they've changed, become less prudish and freer somehow, but on the first day they're all a little nervous.

I sit down and read another chapter of *Stranger in a Strange Land* by Heinlein. The new century is such a confusing time for everyone. I wonder how it'll all shake out, with the new war, technology, pandemics, global warming. It's a lot to ponder. I hear Donahue hobble out and begin his spiel.

"Good morning. I'm Mr. Donahue and this is freshman drawing for Section D. To answer your first question: I had polio as a kid, and I can't walk without my crutches. I'm used to it. It's not a big deal. This year we'll be doing a lot of figure drawing. I see everyone has newsprint pads and soft pencils or charcoal." He looks around at the assembled group beaming. "You're going to use a lot of paper this year. This is just the first of many pads you'll be buying. You have to draw a lot of bodies of all different shapes and sizes to understand what you're seeing and learn to depict the human figure."

I love listening to Donahue talk. He's had a rough life between the polio and his family troubles. He's shared his story of growing up with family members in jail intermittently—his dad for burglary, his brother for manslaughter, and his sister for receiving stolen goods. But he sees only beauty. He put himself through art school playing pool and poker, so I guess the apple doesn't fall far from the tree, but he's a wonderful artist. Sometimes he draws me during class and gives me the sketches. I can look at them as my visual history from a svelte young woman to my present middle-aged rounded self. He still looks at me the same way though, with kindness. I love that.

"This is not a beauty contest," he continues. "The bodies you'll sketch will be young, old, fat and skinny. Your first few hundred drawings will be execrable. Don't worry about it. Learning to portray the human form is something artists have struggled with since the caves at Lascaux; earlier even. It is a skill anyone can learn with practice, and you'll get a lot of practice this year. Keep drawing. Your drawings will get better in time."

"Mr. Donahue will you grade every drawing?" A kid asks.

"Hi. What's your name? I'll learn everyone's name in a week or so. Until then, please introduce yourself," says Donahue.

"I'm Kevin Harris."

"Hi, Kevin. By the way, you don't have to dress up for class, you know." The kid nods. "I'll just grade the ones that aren't totally abysmal." He smiles at the kid. I can see him go red across his neck. "Okay, Catherine, we're ready to begin."

I know this part by heart, but it gives me a thrill to hear him announce my name every time. It's like being a celebrity; I perform in the tradition of Lady Godiva. I take a few deep breaths and check that my hair is off my neck except for a few artistic tendrils.

I wait a few seconds to build the anticipation. Then I emerge wearing just my Chinese silk robe and an enigmatic smile. I feel the students' eyes following me. This is my biggest entrance of the year, so I make the most of it. They won't pay as much attention to me next time. And the time after that, I'll be furniture. But today, I'm like a force field bending air and light in slow motion, as I saunter to the center of the studio.

I approach the model stand, step up with as much grace as I can manage and sit, opposite Donahue. The platform is about seven feet square and eighteen inches tall with a cube of the same height perched on top. I open my sash and let my robe cascade around me like a sigh, awaiting my instructions.

I can sense the intake of breath from most of the students, rather than hear it. Some try to act uninterested and sophisticated, but I know it's a shock for them, a breathing naked person, not a video or a centerfold in a magazine. These are seventeen- and eighteen-year-old art students who've seen hundreds of paintings or sculptures of nudes in museums and in books, but facing a live naked body is a jolt. Most of their eyes travel none too subtly from my head to my pubic area to determine if I'm a natural redhead. I am. I don't have a clue why they all find this information so fascinating, but I've never modeled for a class that didn't check that fact first thing.

When I started posing nude, I figured I'd be embarrassed and feel exposed, but for some reason I didn't. It felt like the most natural thing in the world, like I was being open and honest with everyone for once, nothing hidden or concealed, but I remain aloof from the kids. The secret is to never talk to the students. Never let them hear your voice.

"I think we'll do a two-hour pose, Catherine, so find a position that's comfortable for you," says Donahue. "Turn a little more toward me and extend your left leg. You can rest your elbow on your knee and your chin on your hand. Is that ok?" I nod. "Perfect."

He turns to the kid, Kevin.

"Can you take this chalk and mark on the stand where Catherine's feet are placed? Indicate where her toes are and the sides of her feet. This'll help her get into the same pose after her breaks."

Kevin looks at Donahue like he's just asked him to cut off his leg, but he does what he's asked without breaking the chalk or looking at me. I've seen a few young men like him before, perfectionists, overly neat and careful of his appearance, totally uptight. Art school loosens up most of them. By senior year, he'll sport a beard, wear his clothes wrinkled and have found his soul. I much prefer him to the tortured artist types. I see one sitting behind Kevin smirking. He's wearing all the right clothes, using all the cool jargon, no doubt, but there's nothing inside. He's all angst and pretension.

Before they start to draw, I concentrate on relaxing each and every joint in my body, one by one, starting at my neck and working down to my toes. If I don't do this, I'll start to stiffen and become very uncomfortable even though I get a break every fifteen minutes. Over time, I've learned how to sit or stand so that I can find the exact same position after my break, as well as remain fairly comfortable during the pose.

That's why Donahue keeps asking me to model. I'm no Baywatch beauty and it's not rocket science, but I'm good at my job. During the semester, I'll be back eight or nine times. Donahue likes to bring in a male model, Eddie, who is super skinny, occasionally. There's another female model from Trinidad and one from Sweden, he uses too.

Some of these students walk into art school possessing amazing technical skills; others are admitted with a lot of desire. When I've been away from the class a couple of weeks, it's interesting how some will develop proficiency and others very little. Who will become famous painters or sculptors and who will find desire is not enough? I can't tell. But now, on the first day, no one is disillusioned, no one has found his limits, no one has reached her potential and found it wanting. Desire and optimism reign supreme today.

Also, I usually try to avoid eye contact with the students. I discovered, early on, it rattles them. This kid, Kevin accidentally locks eyes with me and looks away quickly. I feel like I've been accused of something.

I close my eyes and consider what Heinlein wrote about his hero, Valentine Smith, as a super-intelligent creature come to earth and walking among us, while I listen to the scrape, scrape of the charcoal pencils on newsprint all around me. It sounds like the andante, the slowest part of a symphony, restful and comforting.

Layered over the sounds of drawing, I detect another noise. I raise my eyelids and scan the group of students in front of me without moving my head.

I see it. It's Kevin, sharpening his pencil. I watch him work it around and around, as the pencil gets shorter and shorter while a noticeable pile of shavings grows beneath him on the floor.

Donahue is trolling the class, observing everyone's first efforts, but saying nothing. It's not as creepy as it sounds; he's a nice guy. On the first day, he is the objective observer. In later classes, he'll chat with each one, make suggestions and comments. He'll have weekly critiques in which drawings of me from different viewpoints will be pinned up for review. I'm used to it now, but at first I found it strange to see thirty sketches of me on one wall.

He hovers over Kevin's shoulder for a minute and whispers something in his ear. The kid turns red, again, poor thing, and starts to perspire visibly. I see little melon slices of sweat grow under his arms. He stands up and lurches out of the studio, pencil stub in hand.

I glance over and see Donahue grinning like a kid.

I let myself drift back to Heinlein's ideas about a dystopian world where there are no wars, and consider ordering a Waldorf salad for lunch today. I can tell it's getting close to my break and I'm looking forward to standing up. As easy as it might seem to pose sitting still for fifteen minutes, it's difficult and strains your muscles. I make it a habit to schedule regular massages and a yoga class weekly to stay flexible.

Kevin slinks back in, sits on his stool and starts drawing on his newsprint pad. He barely looks at me, but I can hear his pencil scratch against the paper. Donahue calls time a few minutes later and I stand, slip on my robe, and stretch. I walk around the perimeter of the platform a few times to ease the kinks out of my knees and hips before I step down to floor level. It's turned out to be a beautiful sunny day, the temperature's just right in the studio, even for naked ladies.

A girl who must have been sitting behind almost cuts me off trying to reach Kevin, as I head for my cubicle. I slow down and pretend to look at a student drawing to find out what the big emergency is.

"Kevin, what did Mr. Donahue say to you?" she demands.

He sighs and shakes his head looking at the floor. "He said only drawing students or models were allowed in his classroom. If I didn't draw, I'd have to strip naked and pose up there."

"He was probably joking. Do you think he meant it?" I can see she's suppressing a smile.

"I certainly wasn't going to challenge him."

There's one every year. I continue to my cubicle for a sip of tea and to read a few more pages during my break. The first day is always my favorite.

Honor Walk, A Noble Act of Humanity

by LUCY RODRIGUEZ-HANLEY

A few weeks before the world shut down, an Honor Walk was announced over the PA system at my new job. It was the second one that month and the last one due to the pandemic.

The first one was on Valentine's Day. My coworker explained that when an organ donor is about to be taken off life support, the hospital holds an Honor Walk where staff gathers to pay respect to the patient and their family. She asked if I wanted to go, I was embarrassed to tell her that I was afraid of death. I hid behind my bosses' busy schedules as an excuse not to attend.

Six years earlier, I fled my mother's side days before she died. I was not ready for the finality of seeing her wheeled out of her house in a coroner's bag. When my dear friend was dying from a rare salivary cancer, I was not physically there either. It was easier to pretend Mami was alive in New Jersey and Michele in Berkeley. At forty years old, I had not experienced death or the grief that goes with it.

I hesitated before using my badge to open the double doors that lead to the halls of the operating room. I didn't know if I was ready to see someone about to be disconnected from life support. My son spent the first 50 days of his life connected to life supporting machines in the Neonatal Intensive Care Unit at UCLA. He is now a healthy three-year-old but the twitch in my left eye from the PTSD of his early days still lingers. A nurse sensed my discomfort, "You're about to witness a noble act of humanity." she said. I was hypnotized by her words and followed her in a trance.

My spirit crumbled when my son was extubated at two days old and had to be intubated again that night. I was hand expressing breast milk in his small pod when the wires he was hooked up to sounded the loudest alarms of his entire NICU stay. The team of neonatologists, respiratory therapists and nurses rushed to his isolette, someone instructed my sister to take me back to my room. I temporarily blacked out. At some point, I got a call from Charlie's nurse saying he was stable. I asked my nurse for the Percocet I had declined for the C-section pain, hoping it would numb the hopelessness I was feeling.

After Charlie overcame his health issues associated with being born at twenty-eight weeks, I committed myself to live a more purposeful life. I left a lucrative job that did not fulfill my need to contribute to the greater good. I transitioned from working as an Executive Assistant at a Private Equity firm in West Los Angeles to the Executive Assistant of the CEO and COO at my local hospital.

I stood in the crowded hallway outside the operating room along with other hospital staff: Executives, nurses, doctors, and frontline personnel. I listened to their small talk as we hugged the wall behind us to make sure there was ample space for the patient and the family to get through.

I sang *Head, Shoulders, Knees and Toes* in my head when the room started to spin, and the palm of my hands began to sweat. It's the lullaby I soothed my five-year-old daughter with when she was a baby and what I calm myself with whenever anxiety threatens to swallow me. As I finished the song, the elevator doors opened, and a wave of silence fell over the hallway. The wheels of the gurney squeaked and the machines the patient was still hooked up to beeped. I was transported back to the NICU; faking wanting to be there when all I desired was my life to go back to normal. I was a bad friend and a bad daughter. I was not going to add bad mother to my growing list of emotional failures. I had to be there for my son, even when I wanted to run away.

When the second elevator doors opened, I heard the sighs, deep breaths, and stifled cries of the patient's family. A woman said loud Thank Yous in between sobs.

Three people in scrubs wheeled him, one in the front, one in the back and one on the side of the bed. The family walked behind.

I was a few steps from the elevator, but it took what felt like a minute for him to be wheeled past me. I made it a point to look at him, I was there to honor him. I held my breath when I saw how young he was, somewhere between twenty-five and forty. He wore an oxygen mask and an ash cross on his forehead. My reminder that it was Ash Wednesday and another year had passed without me going to mass.

"For dust you are and to dust you shall return." Is what the Catholic priests say when they paint crosses on foreheads with the ashes from the palms of the previous year's Palm Sunday celebration. I had not participated in the ritual since Mami died, it felt like I was inviting death to administer my last rites.

The woman stopped in front of me. "His name is *Jaime Romero, Thank You." She repeated loudly, over and over, making sure everyone knew Jaime's name. She attempted to hide her pain behind an impeccable mask of makeup, but her mascara was running and her pink lipstick was almost gone. Two men followed slowly behind her. The older man looked straight ahead, his ash cross fading from wiping sweat off his forehead with a white handkerchief. The younger one kept his head down, hands folded behind his back. When they turned left towards the operating room, the beeps from the machine subsided and I was finally able to exhale.

I spent my lunch break in the chapel. I prayed for Jaime and his family and hoped they found comfort in knowing his gift will affect one or several lives. I also prayed for a young mom I knew from a NICU support group. After her baby passed away, she pumped milk for other NICU babies so her daughter's short stay on earth made a difference in the lives of others.

When my body failed to make milk for my son during the first three weeks of his life, a stranger donated the liquid gold that sustained him at a crucial time in his development. I hoped the milk came from an over producing mom but the possibility that the milk that nourished my baby was from a mom who lost hers was always in the back of my mind.

After I said my prayers, instead of leaving, I took a place in the back of the line where the chaplain dispensed ashes. I thought about what I was going to focus on during Lent. No more hiding from death. I was ready to come to grips with the fact that Mami and Michele were no longer here. I planned to properly mourn and acknowledge my losses. For Lent last year, I took up honoring grief.

I did not foresee the plot twist that was to come. Was the universe mocking me? The year I chose to honor grief, the Corona Virus was unleashed and life as we knew it changed.

By St. Patrick's Day, my hometown of New York City was hit hard by a worldwide pandemic that had yet to reach California. Friends I knew growing up lost parents, grandparents, aunts and uncles. Zoom funerals and virtual memorial services were part of the new normal. Writing condolence messages two to three times a day for friends and acquaintance was the least I could do to show my support.

Part of what got me through the early days of my mother's death were the many friends who took me to lunch or dinner, who went to museums or hiked with me. I couldn't provide the same type of support to friends whose parents died in hospitals and nursing homes across the country because we were not allowed to gather.

A few days later, the hospital I work at was mostly empty because the Governor's Safer at Home orders included hospitals to shut down elective procedures. People, fearful of catching the virus, also stayed home even when they were not well.

I held it together as best as I could. I exercised before work and prayed that my son and daughter would stay healthy when I dropped them off at daycare.

As the death toll from COVID-19 climbed, I wondered about the other deaths indirectly caused by the pandemic. By April of 2020, organ transplants decreased by fifty percent in the United States according to a news release in Penn Medicine News. The vanished hopes of those on waitlists for life-saving organ transplants were another casualty of the pandemic.

A year has passed and 60,000 people have died in California. The number of infections is down but the death toll is still climbing. I think of Jaime's family often. Are they grateful he died when he did? Had he lived longer, they would not have been able to visit him, donate his organs or walk him to his final destination in the operating room.

With so many losses and collective grief over the last year, I have finally accepted that my mother and Michele are gone and I chose to miss the opportunity to say a last goodbye. I am grateful that I was able to be at my mother's bedside until anxiety and fear of life without her dictated that I couldn't. I think of my resilient friends who said goodbye to loved ones over an iPad, and the frontline workers who witnessed so much death. I feel guilty for the advance notice I got when my mother was diagnosed with cancer. I spent seven years righting the wrongs in our relationship. I didn't think Mami or Michele would die and when they did, it was easier to pretended they were still with me. Their deaths and the grief I hid from gave me strength and allowed me to be present for my son when he needed me the most.

* Name has been changed to protect the family's privacy.

The Book of Generation(s) of the Negress

by ASHUNDA NORRIS

from *LA PRESA*

I begat myself
in rose water myrrh & rum

eden : my hair follicle
shedding spells & grace

behold! afro halo
wild & becoming

I : mania of holy
golden framed & cannabis oiled

10,000 times I have
anointed & 10,000

shall serve me
with benevolence & new nations

I am the supreme
knowledge eve curved into

her sons as she lay dying
of ribbed oaths

if my womb never answers
a desire still, I am

the god from which they all came

She is a friend of my mind. She gather me, man. The pieces I am, she gather them and give them back to me in all the right order.

Toni Morrison

The Other Tattoo

by JENISE MILLER

from *RAISING MOTHERS*

i first saw it
after a nurse scanned
my mother's skin
under a blue light
searching for a vein
to insert a new lifeline
where illness
swelled her arms
and hands as she laid
unconscious

i already knew
my father's last name
inked on one hand
though i never asked
when how or where
she got it did she hide it
from her mother
did her mother find out
and disapprove

my mother who told me
not to wear make-up
questioned the length
and fit of my skirt
even though old photos revealed
a woman who wore cherry red
lipstick on full lips and strutted
long-legged in cut off shorts

now the doctors search
for clues and a cause
was it the cancer

that returned
or the ailments
stacked against her
in this moment

of stillness and searching
i notice another tattoo
i look close to read
letters that perhaps were
once black, now faded green
and i imagine

someone other than
the woman i've known
all of my life
but only part of hers
and i want more time

to know her
the woman she was
before any expectations to be
more than who she wanted to be

i want more time
to know the woman
with another tattoo

her own blessed name
on her body

Mastectomy, Simple

by BONNIE S. KAPLAN

from *BELLEVUE LITERARY REVIEW*

I never expected to feel the cool drink running
so close to my skin, just under my newly sutured
chest, my heart side now genderless and tender—

to love my flat chest, so much like the one I had at 13,
skateboarding in t-shirts without a bra. Never expected
to notice my right nipple, how it still becomes hard—

a lonely pleasure like that of an only child.
Never expected to forsake the idea
of a matched set, how someone could rest their head

on my left chest, tuck in like a baby to its father,
hear the oscillation of my heartbeat, just beneath
the surface, resonant fountain, chamber music.

Revival Theater

by SANDY YANG

from *MANY MOUNTAINS MOVING*

Ten days before her wedding, Lydia still hadn't ordered a cake. Brendan had originally asked her to book the photographer, but changed his mind when she suggested a friend who used to photograph child soldiers in Sierra Leone. And now Brendan refused to go to the bakeries on her list, just because one of them mentioned "erotic desserts" on its website, as if Lydia would order a penis-shaped cake just to spite him.

Finally, they drove to a bakery in Newport Beach whose color scheme alternated between cream and eggshell. Brendan pointed to a wedge of chalky cake behind the curved glass display.

"White is a color, not a flavor," Lydia said. "A chocolate cake would taste much better."

"People will get chocolate in their teeth, and who's going to pay to get that photoshopped?"

"Yeah, we'd look like we're eating roaches and poo."

"Is everything a joke with you?" he asked, looking at her through rimless glasses, as disappointed as Lydia's father had been when she was a girl. "It's a joke, right, that you wanted a war photographer to shoot our wedding?"

They headed back home after Brendan ordered the lemon cake. He must have felt guilty because he turned on to Pacific Coast Highway without Lydia asking him to take the scenic route. She looked out the window and watched the blurry white line separating the sky from the ocean, heaven from earth, or just two slightly different shades of blue. She wished it could go on forever, but the sky was already darkening and they would soon arrive in their apartment.

A year ago, Lydia watched the same view from the backseat of a car that her married couple friends were driving. By the time they reached Malibu for the hike, they met up with another couple who also brought their single friend.

Brendan was clean-cut and worked in corporate America, the type of guy the folks would love if Lydia had folks, the kind who prompted people to wonder out loud why he wasn't attached. But he answered that question the moment he opened his mouth, correcting people for misusing "I" for "me," inquiring if they were colorblind for wearing the wrong seasonal color. Still, Lydia had never met anyone who watched the obscure documentaries they'd only show at the revival theater, the same dark space where she must have sat near him before they even met.

Over the years, people had also said to her, "You're so lovely, how can you be single?"

Sometimes, Lydia wondered if she was marrying Brendan to avoid the question, since she would end up confiding that the love of her life had been taken far too soon. If they pressed further, she'd smile and tell them that it was still too painful to talk about.

The truth being that it happened when she was young.

And it wasn't a person. It was a pair of woodpeckers.

Lydia had lived in Seattle with her parents until the car crash left her an orphan at five years old. She was the one who had begged them to drive to the video store that rainy day after they had argued all afternoon. Lydia hadn't cared about the Disney movie she'd thrown a fit over. She only wanted to stop her parents from fighting and to see her friends, the woodpeckers, again.

Perhaps they were just wipers, but in the rain Piyu and Pecker came to life, as if the windshield were their stage. Pecker always poked his pointy head up first, followed by Piyu, who got his name because he was always getting a whiff of Pecker's butt and saying "pee-yu." He explained this to Lydia when they first said hello and immediately started cracking jokes.

"What do you want to do right now?" they asked her in unison that day.

"I want to fly away," Lydia said.

"Ah yes, flying was a grand old time, remember, Pecker," said Piyu, who whipped himself into a frenzy, clearing the gauze of rainwater that kept smearing the view of the road ahead.

"You're woodpeckers," Lydia pointed out. "You *can* fly away anytime you want, so why are you stuck here?"

"We are not stuck," Pecker said. "We're eating rain for breakfast."

"Yum," Lydia said, just as Piyu started singing.

"In one hole, out the other, easy on the drinks," he squawked out a tune. "Cuz pee-yuuu, man, your butt really stinks."

Lydia's mother turned her head back from the passenger seat.

"What're you laughing at, sweetie?" she asked, sounding tired.

In a few moments, Pecker had stopped singing. He lay motionless against the windshield as if he had been bobbing his head above water all this time only to slip quietly beneath its surface. The rain quickly obstructed the view on her father's side. He swore and gripped the steering wheel, his knuckles hard and exposed. Her mother urged him to pull into the parking lot of the liquor store up ahead, and for once, he listened. After he parked and stepped out of the car, Lydia watched his blurred figure hover over the windshield, and before she understood what he was doing, her father grabbed Pecker, yanking him so hard he broke his neck. Lydia screamed, watching her friend dangle in the air from a hinge.

She wanted to run outside, but the door was locked. She

pulled and pulled at the handle until a piece of the plastic broke off.

"Look what you did," her mother yelled at her now, as if resuming the fight they had left behind in the house, except that in the place of her father was Lydia.

When her father returned to the car, he was holding Pecker in one hand, and Lydia lunged forward and reached for him. Her mother slapped her and told her to sit down, but Lydia had managed to touch the very tip of Pecker. He was cold and rubbery, like he was dead. Her father threw him in the trunk and slammed it shut.

"I hate you, I hate you, I hate you," Lydia yelled until she wore out her voice.

Just how her father lost control of the car after he drove off the parking lot, she didn't know, but she remembered Piyu urging her to look at the view he was clearing just for her. She wiped her eyes and did what he asked. All around, lights illuminated the raindrops. She remembered the lit store signs, the car blinkers, but most of all, the stoplights that appeared fractured and dreamlike, as if glowing pieces of red, yellow and green had lost their way and attached themselves to puddles along the road, creating entryways into another dimension.

It began to rain on Pacific Coast Highway, and Brendan immediately flicked the bar to the right of the steering wheel. The wipers streaked dust and condensation across the windshield, as the drizzle soon fattened into raindrops, beating a steady rhythm on the roof of the car.

He put a hand on Lydia's knee. Navigating a rain-soaked mountain road with only his left hand was apparently his way of saying sorry.

Now it was her duty to diffuse the tension so he could put two hands back on the wheel again, not compromise their safety, the rest of their lives together. She pretended not to notice and kept looking straight out of the bleary window, at the wipers whipping back and forth, where the one on the right seemed to wink, as if to say, "What do you want to do right now?"

The rain kept coming.

Eventually, Brendan's touch began to drift from her knee, but before he could withdraw completely, Lydia took his hand and held on to it for as long as he would let her.

El Arroyo

by ROBERTA H. MARTÍNEZ

SYNOPSIS

In 1924 JULITA and her husband HUMBERTO, are expecting their first child. Will they secure their dreams in their home beside el arroyo?

CHARACTERS

JULITA, Mexicana/Latina, mid 20s to 18 to play 15 years old, clothes are simple but very well fitted, old shoes. Hair pulled back from face, her arm is bruised. She is seven or eight months pregnant. Trusting. Wife of HUMBERTO.

LETICIA, Mexicana/Latina, to play 20 years old, clothes similar to JULITA, but not as crisp. Understated, quick on pick up. Friend and Sister-figure to JULITA.

HUMBERTO, Mexicano/Latino, to play early 20s, Slender, wiry build. Husband of JULITA. Cunning. Initially dressed in work clothes. Changes to fine blue shirt with elegant buttons.

TIME

1924, Late Winter

PLACE

La Junta, CO

SETTING

Interior clean, old, simple, adobe house. One side is at an angle, to show exterior of house and narrow, slightly steep arroyo; dirt path on other side.

Door is stage left, two windows stage right. Both windows are set high and have no glass, but have vertical sticks and exterior wooden shutters. Light from window insinuates time of day.

There is no window on upstage wall. Image of Santo Niño de Atocha is clearly visible. Votive candle burning.

Free standing cupboard and cast-iron stove, table, chairs, bed, and cradle are in room.

Bedframe is metal, cover is faded floral print.

SCENE I

At RISE:

Afternoon.

Women are seated at table; coffee pot, two cups and saucers on table.

In distance occasional barking dog.

JULITA

¿Más café?

LETICIA

No, gracias. Your pan dulce is so light and sweet - I don't want to leave a crumb on the plate.

JULITA

We make a little money from selling it. Every bit helps.

LETICIA

It must feel good to see people and talk to them when they buy the pan dulce.

JULITA

Oh, I don't do that. I just leave a basket with the pan in it and a jar for them to leave the money. Humberto gave me the idea and it works! I'm not used to talking to people I don't know. I'm always a little surprised that people come all the way out here to buy it.

LETICIA

Well, of course they would? It smells so good, it's delicious and (in a joking tone) there's no panaderia in this town.

They share a laugh.

JULITA

Being with you reminds of my mother. We'd used to eat pan dulce, drink coffee, and laugh. The hardest thing is not being able to talk to her.

LETICIA

Que en paz descanse. (They cross themselves)

LETICIA notices bruise on JULITA's right arm.

Oh, what is that?

JULITA

What? Oh... (She covers bruise with sleeve)

LETICIA

Yes. Humberto did that to you? I've told you he shouldn't.

JULITA

He gets carried away by his passion. He tries to help me do what's right. My dad did that with my mama and she always did better.

LETICIA

He might hurt the baby.

JULITA

Oh, no, Letty, he's careful. (Motions to belly) He never hits me there. Besides, I started it. I complained about his spending time with Cuca.

LETICIA

Hmph. Going over there to see Cuca and then thinking you won't be upset.

JULITA

I know. It's just the way men are. Besides, I have my ways of getting back at her.

LETICIA

At her? ¿Cómo?

JULITA

Well, you know how Humberto has me cook for them.

LETICIA

(Matter of fact tone) You're cooking for Humberto and Cuca?

JULITA

Only dinner. When he takes the comida to her house he hasn't noticed that sometimes I send over plates that have little chips in them. She may be eating what I cook, but she's not getting my best plates. Ha. So, as I hear him bolt the door...I know that soon she'll know what I think of her.

LETICIA

He bolts the door when he leaves.

JULITA

Uh huh. It's his way of keeping me safe when he's gone.

LETICIA

That's confusing.

JULITA

It's pretty simple. The door is open all day, so I can do my work. At night, when I'm alone, no one can come in with the door bolted. Humberto unbolts the door when comes back at night or in the morning when he comes back for breakfast.

LETICIA

I've heard that Cuca's husband, Fernando, got out of jail...

JULITA

He did?

LETICIA

...and that Cuca might be going back with him.

JULITA

Really? She might take him back?

LETICIA

That's what I've heard. Have you heard that?

JULITA

No, but you're the only one who visits me. I love our time together. Sometimes I get lonely.

LETICIA

You know sometimes I worry about you, out here...by yourself. And Humberto...

JULITA

Beat.

Looks to window.

It's getting late.

JULITA rises from chair.

Humberto will be getting off work soon. I need to start cooking dinner. Thank you for the baby clothes and the... embroidered coverlet will keep our baby so warm.

LETICIA

It is getting late. I'll come again before the baby comes. I only...

JULITA

Thank you. (All but pushes LETICIA outdoor) Again.

LETICIA leaves to walk on path.

JULITA stokes fire in stove and begins to cut vegetables.

SCENE II

At RISE:

Almost dusk, light coming in from window.

HUMBERTO enters happy and full of energy, striding cross the Arroyo, and taking rise with ease, we lose sight of him as he walks behind the windowless wall, and then he exuberantly enters through the door.

HUMBERTO

Chulita. Querida. Where is my Chulita? Hmmm, smells good.

JULITA

I'm here, Humberto.

HUMBERTO

Kisses her on the forehead.

Ah, Princesa. Mi Princesa.

Touches her pregnant belly.

Moving today?

JULITA

Yes. Not, too much, but, a little. All this time and I'm still not used to it. I can barely wait to hold our baby.

HUMBERTO

Me, too. (Gently taps her belly, she recoils slightly) Soon, m'ijo, soon.

JULITA

Hope he looks like you. He'll be so handsome and strong.

During following dialogue she goes to stove, cooks tortillas, and places cooked tortillas in dish towel.

He taps cradle as he goes to a tin that holds water, takes off his shirt, wipes his face and under his arms. He picks up a folded shirt and buttons the shirt while talking.

HUMBERTO

Notices cups and saucer stacked on cupboard.

(Casually) What's this?

JULITA

Letty came over today. I love when she visits.

HUMBERTO

So why were you talking to Leticia?

JULITA

She says I may only have a month or two before the baby's born. She brought the baby clothes that she's not using anymore.

HUMBERTO

Did she think we couldn't buy new clothes for our son? Why do you have to go around making people think that we can't buy new things?

JULITA

It wasn't that way. We spent time talking about things I don't know like...what it's like to have a baby in the house.

HUMBERTO

I don't want her visiting when I'm not here. Understand?

JULITA

But, it's just...

HUMBERTO

Moving towards her.

Do you understand?

JULITA nods.

Do you understand?

JULITA

Yes.

HUMBERTO

Yes?

JULITA

Yes, Humberto.

HUMBERTO

(Tone changes, becoming affable) Well, now, what's for dinner? Smells delicious.

HUMBERTO looks toward window.

It's almost time for me to go.

JULITA

Places stewpot in a basket on table.

I made albondigas and fresh tortillas.

HUMBERTO

You remembered the besos and conchas.

JULITA

Adds pan dulce.

Of course. I saved some for you.

Smiles as she adds plates, then places her hands on small of back. Quietly expresses discomfort.

HUMBERTO

Hurry up. You know how people hate to wait.

HUMBERTO finishes getting ready, then goes to door. He's oblivious to her discomfort.

I'm ready.

She places blue dishtowel on top of basket, carries it to door and gives it to him.

He goes out door and carefully places basket on a small table beside the door. Closes and bolts door; picks up basket and leaves as he entered.

JULITA goes to door and touches it.

HUMBERTO goes to ravine side; carefully places basket on rock. The goes to window shutter and closes from outside the adobe.

HUMBERTO

Good night. Princesa.

JULITA

Good night, Humberto.

JULITA picks up coverlet from cradle, goes to bed, and cries quietly. Puts hand to back; emits a slow, soft moan.

SCENE III

At RISE

Night time, full moon.

JULITA is asleep on bed, still holding baby's coverlet; bed covering is rumpled.

HUMBERTO, moaning, struggles to crawl up wash. Blood on

shirt; holds his belly.

HUMBERTO

¡Julita! ¡Julita!

JULITA

Sits upright. Looks straight downstage.

Yes, Humberto.

HUMBERTO

¡Ayúdame!

His speech becomes breathier and weaker.

JULITA

What, Humberto?

HUMBERTO

I've been stabbed.

JULITA

¡Ay, Dios! Hay voy, Humberto.

Rushes to door, which is bolted.

Oh, Santo Niño, give me strength.

Tries and can't open.

I'm trying.

Goes to middle of room.

What should I do Humberto? I can barely hear you.

HUMBERTO

Open the window.

JULITA

She goes to window and can't reach.

I can't reach it, Humberto.

HUMBERTO

(Weak but angrily) Cabrona, stand on something!

He looks in disbelief at his wound. Tries to crawl up wash; is in agony and can't.

It's warm...it won't stop. This can't be.

JULITA drags chair to window and stands on it, after she grabs the palote.

HUMBERTO

(In disbelief) Estoy muriendo.

JULITA begins to hit the window shutters with palote. They open. His sounds are clearer.

HUMBERTO

No. My son, I won't see my son!

JULITA

Humberto! Don't say that. ¡Por favor!

Tries hitting rails with palote one more time, loses balance, and falls off footstool.

HUMBERTO

Ayúdame, Julita... I need you...

JULITA

She tries to get up; leg of footstool gives.

I'm trying.

Gets second chair; tries again, chair falls.

HUMBERTO

Ayúdame. (Several beats, then he reaches up, not clear if it's to sky or to JULITA). Ayú...

JULITA

Places hands on back, makes guttural sound.

It hurts. What's happening? (Gasps, looks at floor). I'm wet?

She bends over still holding her back.

Only wind and her soft moans are heard.

Light changes - night with moon to dawn.

LETICIA seen running up road to the adobe.

SCENE IV

At RISE:

Light on road leading to house; house is dark.

Rooster crows.

LETICIA

Julita, Julita! Cuca's husband Fernando came back! They're saying he stabbed Humberto. Julita...

JULITA

(In dark, sobs deeply) Tanta sangre, tanta sangre...

LETICIA

Julita, are you okay?

LETICIA struggles to unbolt door. Flings it open, light on JULITA who is holding a form in the coverlet, which is soaked in blood.

JULITA seated rocking from side to side on chair by cradle.

JULITA

(In a sing-song chant) Están muertos, muertos, muertos. Están muertos, muertos, muertos. Están muertos...

Her bloody hand reaches out to LETICIA, who goes to her and rocks her as lights dim.

LETICIA

Shhh, shhh, shh...

Mourning dove nest call.

SOUND: link for closing song/birds sound: https://www.allaboutbirds.org/guide/Mourning_Dove/sounds

Black.

We cannot change the world alone. To heal ourselves, to restore the earth to life, to create the situations in which freedom can flourish, we must work together in groups.

Starhawk

Eviction Blues

by NATALIE SMITH PARRA

from *DRYLAND* and *HIP MAMA*

I'm standing at the sink washing dishes and mindlessly half-gazing out the kitchen window. Sabine the Lizard Woman walks by with a huge iguana draped across her shoulder and carrying a desert tortoise in each hand. She sees me through the window and attempts an awkward wave, and I attempt one back with my soapy-bubble-covered hand.

Today a prospective buyer came to see my place. Susan-the-landlord had given me 24 hours notice as required by law, but I hadn't bothered cleaning the kitchen before they got here, and now I'm glad. I hadn't been worried about the potential buyer or the sale of my place in general. I believed that anyone with the money to buy this big triplex property (income property!) would never live in this neighborhood. They'll be investors, I thought, and we have rent control in L.A., so it shouldn't affect me however it goes.

I LOVE MY EAST HOLLYWOOD APARTMENT WITH ITS HIGH CEILINGS, LONG HALLWAY, WORN HARDWOOD FLOORS, THE BIG DINING ROOM WITH A CAFÉ DOOR TO THE KITCHEN.

My family and I had painted it ourselves: Frida-Kahlo-house-blue kitchen, dining room the color of the inside of a mango, deep sealing-wax-red for the hallway. I walk everywhere and have been content to live mostly within the proverbial two-mile radius around their home that many people seldom leave. There are two historic movie theaters within a mile, two bookstores that have lasted through time, one with a café. The neighborhood vacillates between identities. If you come in from the west, you've arrived in Thai Town. From the east, you're in Little Armenia. This is the only home Elisa remembers. Her friends are an eclectic gang of Russian, Mexican and Jamaican kids who spend the days kicking a soccer ball in my small fenced front yard, the only grass on our block, or devising ways to get enough money to buy cheap outfield seats for the night games at Dodger Stadium and cajoling an adult to take them. Yegor, the little Russian boy who loves Elisa, writes on her birthday card, "I wish you health and good friends. I wish you everything perfect, just the way you want it."

The duplex has sheltered me through my cancer diagnosis (You'll be dead in four months!), two lung surgeries in four months, chemotherapy, radiation. Years from now, I will look back at what most people think would have been the worst years of my life, but I'll think of mostly the good times: walking in old Hollywood with my son, Jonathon and stopping to have our picture taken and transferred to a felt calendar, all of us huddled together in my bedroom hiding from a mouse with a towel stuffed under the door. "What if it comes in through the bathroom?" Elisa asked, Sara's hot pink hair in a time when no one had hot pink hair, big Thanksgivings, even bigger Christmas parties. Elisa practicing Ode to Joy on the secondhand piano.

I'D HOPED I WOULD LIVE HERE FOREVER, AND I'D FORGOTTEN FOR A WHILE THAT THE ONLY THING CAPITALISM OFFERS US IN ABUNDANCE IS CHANGE, AND IT'S USUALLY NOT GOOD.

The prospective buyer arrived in a black BMW. It was around noon, but she wore a black dress and stiletto heels. Her entourage followed her into the house: a loan officer in a silver-gray skirt suit, a curly-haired assistant balancing camera equipment and notebooks, a real estate agent. When I opened the door she introduced herself as Michelle. Her eyes were shifty and focused behind me when I extended my hand. No one opened a closet or turned on a faucet. Good, I thought. An investor. She'll be my new landlord, and who cares. I hope she lives far away. I sat on the sofa and watched them bounce from room to room, snapping angles of my house with an expensive camera. "Oh look, Michelle!" one of them says, "She's painted every room a different color!" They're in my bedroom now. "How cu-u-u-te! Doesn't she look comfortable? Hi, kitty! Kiss kiss kiss!" Later I will see someone's skinny ass print on my down comforter, where they sat to pet the cat. "Look at these nice furnishings!" the assistant says, and runs her hand over my gorgeous forest green bookshelves.

A writer from Montana who I met at Mesa Refuge shook his head in disbelief when I talked about my community in East Hollywood, and at least two, maybe three, books published by writers in my Silver Lake fiction writers' group scorned East Hollywood as the Hell's Kitchen of the west coast, a place worthy only of criminals and castoffs.

The day after Michelle and her cohort invade my house, Susan calls early, as if she'd been waiting by the phone and watching the clock. She needs to see me right away, and in that moment, I realize I will not be growing old in my East Hollywood place. Susan arrives in a big red SUV and parks it blocking the driveway. She is pale and her lips are dry. I know there is a big money deal on the table, I can tell, but Susan comes to me as my benefactor. She will let me stay in the house until June, even though the lease is up in May, to let Elisa finish the school year. She asks me to sign a letter she's typed on a manual typewriter. It's full of misspellings and White Out and says I agree to move out on June fifteenth. There is a hand drawn line where my signature goes.

"Are you out of your mind, Susan? Why would I sign this?" This is the first time Susan and I have been less than cordial with each other. She and her husband are good landlords, if you don't consider good landlord an oxymoron. They don't raise the rent, they fix what needs to be fixed, and she always drops off a birthday present for Elisa. It does need mentioning that I've paid more than 80,000 dollars of her mortgage, and that should count for something. She has generally stayed out of my business and I've stayed out of hers, except when I send the rent check, always on time.

"YOU HAVE NO CHOICE," SUSAN SAYS. "THIS IS MY PROPERTY AND I CAN DO WHAT I WANT."

Of course, I know this, but I also know there are legal proceedings to eviction. There are rules, there's a rent stabilization board, there is relocation money for displaced tenants.

"Look," I say, "if the buyer wants to evict me, she can do it after escrow closes with a legal eviction notice and a five thousand dollar relocation fee."

I whine to my friend Frank on the phone. He's also living under the eviction gun, but in San Francisco.

"You've made that place as good as anyone can make it, but let's face it, that neighborhood...it's..."

"A slum." I finish his sentence.

"Yea, a slum," he repeats.

But that doesn't help. I will mourn for my neighborhood: the Armenian vegetable seller blowing a horn to the tune of La Cucaracha in the mornings, the Lizard Woman with her large collection of reptiles—including water dragons, five-foot-long iguanas and 35 various tortoises—who lives with her boyfriend, a Batman memorabilia collector, each one complaining about the other's hobby. I'll miss next door neighbor Liz who goes out bundled up early Saturday mornings to sell the *Revolutionary Worker* in the garment district. I'll miss Javier and Mateo and their pug Charlie. I may even miss Jumbo's Clown Room Nude Nude Nude, and the smell of urine on Hollywood Boulevard. But I live under capitalism, and it's now time to move on.

The day after Susan's visit, still stunned from the news, I walk to Espreso mi Cultura to drink coffee and feel sorry for myself. I turn onto Western and a rat the size of a smallish cat darts in front of me and disappears under a bougainvillea vine growing up a fence. I hate rodents. I'm terrified of them, but for the first time, a rat makes me smile a little. I wish it luck. Go with God, little rat. Que le vaya bien.

When Mama Sang the Blues

by ANGELA M. FRANKLIN

from *CULTURAL WEEKLY* and *PORTSIDE*

I hated the blues because
Daddy hated them more.
He came home from work.
The 33's spinning under diamond tips.
Mama nursing a cold one instead
of shoving cornbread into a hot oven
or sautéing onions for smothered steak.

Mama's blues came by invitation
liberation flowed through
gold-capped teeth.
Blues stole my mama
made her backtalk her angry
man. Whoever said a black woman
was always liberated
didn't walk in my Mama's heels.

Her blues erupted like crude oil
in the middle of a pristine lake without notice.
Mama nursed a black eye after salty talk
crushed Schlitz cans
stacked on our dining table instead of dinner.

Topics Over Time with You

by KARIN AURINO

from *RED ROCK REVIEW*

A police chief tries to shake us down when we bury a friend in a foreign country while I am seven months pregnant with our daughter.

Classical music plays at the Hollywood Bowl where you kick the bottle of red and it splashes on my white linen pants.

On September 11 you get dressed for work and I hold our one-year-old daughter while we watch the twin towers live on the news.

I pack artfully decorated lunch bags with tasty nourishments when you go to work and thecomp any bans food in the offices.

After my heart stops briefly on the table our son is born and he will grow into a fine teenager who starts an online gaming club through his high school with his friends and his science teacher during the COVID-19 pandemic.

My cousin has hemophilia but our family only recently finds out he contracted AIDS as a teenager in the 80's while receiving a blood transfusion after an accident.

The doctor finds a lump in my breast in the same week that my asthmatic sister contracts the virus and it takes so long to find out if it will kill us.

Our children live with us during the pandemic and we have a little party when our daughter turns twenty.

Uncle Bob dies from Coronavirus after a long summer of suffering
and I remember all the times my sisters and I spent playing
on his dairy farm when we were little.

His wife survives.
We survive.

Time Travel

by TONI ANN JOHNSON

from *SPROUT MAGAZINE* and republished in *RED FEZ* and *ARLIJO*

Twenty-one years later I'll run into you outside the Path Station in Hoboken in front of the wide green awning that leads down to the trains. Sounds of rumbling below and the din of chatter swirling, you'll yell my name above the noise, saying it like a question, as if you could actually be unsure that it's me.

I'll turn and totter on the top step. Just in time. Seconds later and I'd be swept into the stream of bodies flowing to the tracks.

It'll be shortly after 5pm on a late September weekday, humid and sunny, with air that smells of commuters caught in unexpected high heat. Perspiration will roll down my back and leak between the butt cheeks you used to make fun of.

I'll squint against the sun and stare at you. You'll smile with closed lips and brown eyes that'll be gentler than I'll remember. Several seconds will pass before you'll say, "Wow. First time I've ever seen you away from home. Where're you living these days?"

"Manhattan," I'll say.

"Oh. The big city," you'll say, like it's a truly good thing.

I'll nod. I won't ask you anything. I'll look at you and wait.

Suits of blue, black, gray, and tan will dodge and whoosh past us in both directions. Heels clicking on concrete, huffs and impatient scoffs; we'll be in the way.

I'll shield my eyes with one hand and be silent for so long it'll feel impolite. You'll hold a cheap gray suit jacket over one shoulder, your white collared shirt bearing sweat marks under the arms. You'll smell of Obsession For Men, alluring and more sophisticated than the Old Spice I used to notice at the bus stop during high school, when you rarely spoke to me. Your chest will be broad and you'll be slim, like me, which will mean something, because twenty-one years earlier we were chubby six-year-olds foraging together for Ding Dongs and Oreos my mother hid deep in the pantry so we wouldn't overeat. We'd find them, and eat them all, and that thrill was a bond we shared.

But being connoisseurs of Nabisco Cookies and Hostess Snack Cakes, and being buddies from the time we could crawl, never made our bond as strong as the one you shared with every kid in the neighborhood but me.

Someone'll bump into you and you'll fall into me and grab my arm before I lose my balance on the top step.

"Sorry. You alright?" you'll ask.

I'll say, "Fine, thanks." And take my arm back.

That day, twenty-one years after I lost you, I'll be wearing a tomato-red kufi atop unapologetically kinky hair—wild kinks I tamed the soul out of when I lived across the street from you, hoping straight hair would make me pretty, and more like everyone else. But you called me an ugly, bubble-butted nigger at the bus stop. Elementary school became junior high, which turned into high school and I barely existed. You had all those years to speak to me. That day I'll wonder, why now?

I'll have on black chunky boots and a dress that's lime-green, like LifeSavers candies. Red, black, and green are Pan-African colors and I'll wear them because at the time, I'll be mad and militant, saying fuck you to you and everyone else from home who said my color, my hair, and my big butt made me ugly. That day at the Path Station it won't matter to me that you were only a boy when you said those things.

I won't smile. I won't be warm. I'll forget any mean things I may have said back at the bus stop. I probably said some, because I *will* remember how you winced at the mention of your fat mom, crippled father, and port-wine stain birth-marked baby sister. My tongue, sharpened on figurative and literal sticks and stones hurled at me by neighborhood bullies must have pierced your soft spots sometimes, too. Yet you'll look at me that day with a tenderness that insists cruel words never passed between us.

Your dark hair will be short. Your skin clean-shaven, clear, the spots of adolescence healed and faded. Your face will flush and your eyes will brighten the way they used to shine when you were my round-cheeked running buddy. You'll look deep into me with such warmth that against my will you'll begin to melt the icicles that numbed me inside.

My name, when you say it, will sound like songs from playtimes past. In your eyes I'll catch a glimpse of us singing on swings, flying above the grass where we found four-leaf clovers. You'll invite me into a little chamber of your heart where you saved us. But I won't go. I won't be ready to remember how to get there.

There'll be no mention of what happened to us, or what didn't happen that should have. You'll sing my name again, a young boy's sweetness shining out of your grown man's face and you'll say, "You were my first best friend."

I'll know you're telling me you're sorry. You didn't mean to hurt me. You were just a kid.

I'll nod politely and shrug off your words of apology. I'll carry my bubble-butt and my baggage down the stairs, catch my train and move on with my life.

In another twenty-one years, I'll be middle aged and softer inside and out, the rough edges of resentment worn down with experience. I'll remember how you said my name that day and the way you looked at me with affection. I'll transport myself back to the Path Station, in front of the stairs, trains rumbling below, bodies whooshing by, and I'll be kinder to you. I will. Because by then I'll know that love is the only feeling left once enough time has passed.

To build community requires vigilant awareness of the work we must continually do to undermine all the socialization that leads us to behave in ways that perpetuate domination.

bell hooks

Self-Portrait as Angry Flower

by ELLINE LIPKIN

I was the single bud in the vase,
yearning my neck just over the glass.
Meant to drink water
straight up my center.

I was placed in the corner,
maybe table, silent, admired,
unpetaling lilac into white,
scenting, while viscous thick
at the bottom of the glass.

I was meant to be
that decorative, thorn
sheared, just an edge
left sharp. I fleck petals,
belligerent, wet the table
carmine-dark, stew into
a rich, insouciant black.

Promises Are Coffee

by LUIVETTE RESTO

It's Wednesday
and I ask my father
if he can mail me
two packages of coffee
from Puerto Rico.

My request is specific and desperate:
It has to be Café Crema.
My grandmother worked for the company
until she retired in her late 40s.
In between meetings
she created my name on her desk pad.
I can't find this brand in the States.

I ask my father
and he quickly promises with a
Sí, sí por supuesto
and I reply with gratitude
like a daughter would
forgetting the cardless birthdays,
the chances I gave away like bendiciónes
at the end of a phone call
and the afternoons where I waited and waited
like a daughter would.

But today he promises coffee
he knows how much it means to me
and I believe him
like a daughter would
because this kind of coffee
can only be found on the island
just like him.

Nostrand Avenue, between J and K

by JOAN SELIGER SIDNEY

I was the mouse under the table. The dark world of woolen skirts, nylons and heels didn't scare me. The red-checkered oilcloth hung all the way down. I felt safe. All that mattered was the chatter of the women drinking coffee, dunking their biscuits.

Mom lifted the tablecloth. I closed my eyes, hoping she couldn't see me either.

"Little pitchers have big ears," Mom said. "Go play outside."

I put my pointer fingers in my ears. I wouldn't leave.

The women who coffee-klatched were Mom's two sisters or her neighbors. Aunt Luba, my favorite aunt, lived next door. "She's too fat," said Aunt Minka, who lived in the Bronx. "Luba should lose forty pounds. All day she eats sweets."

"Abie likes her that way," Mom said. "'She's *zaftig*,' he says."

I liked her the way she was, too. Under the table I saw how her ankles bulged out of her shoes. Her legs looked like Dumbo's. So what?

Aunt Minka's feet were skinny-skinny. How did her shoes stay on?

"She's so stingy, she starves herself," Aunt Luba said. "She begs the butcher for bones to make soup. He doesn't know she and Yorgie must have a million under their mattress."

"Minka doesn't wash," Mom said. "Probably to save soap."

From my hiding place, I heard everything. Smelled it, too.

Aunt Minka stunk from smelly socks and cigarettes. I thought about Uncle Yorgie. Always a cigarette sticking out of his mouth, too. I thought about Uncle Abie, my favorite uncle. His good idea was to pay me a nickel to pull Uncle Yorgie's tie. I loved our game. Once I started, I wouldn't stop. Yank, yank, yank. Uncle Yorgie didn't find it funny. "Why do you pull my tie?" I kept quiet. How could I tell on Uncle Abie? We both laughed when I came to collect.

From my hiding place, I couldn't say who was fatter: Aunt Luba or Anna Policano, her best friend. She lived on the first floor. My pal Louie was the fifth of her six sons. We walked to school holding hands. The crossing guard liked to say, "Here come Mr. and Mrs. Policano."

Once, from under the table, I heard Louie's mom say, "I'm done. No more trying for a girl."

What did she mean? How do you try for a girl?

I believed Mom when she told me she chose me from all the children in the hospital. "You were so skinny. You looked at me with pleading eyes. I knew I had to take you home. Feed and fatten you up."

But then I heard Mom say, "I'd still like a second child."

"Hurry up," Aunt Luba said. "You're not getting any younger."

"I have to convince Srulik. He says, 'Joanie was so much trouble. One's enough!'"

Trouble?

Another time Mom told me I came six weeks early. She had to leave me with the preemies. "Three times a day I pumped my milk and brought it by bus to the maternity hospital."

Was that my fault? I felt confused. Which story was true? I kept quiet so Mom wouldn't remember I was listening.

I knew I had been "a poor eater." Mom told me she tried "everything." Once she cooked chocolate pudding. When I shut my mouth, she got angry and pulled it open.

"Spoon after spoon I pushed in. You started choking, turned blue. I held you upside down until you began breathing. Never again!"

Dad's right. I wasn't easy.

I still didn't like to eat. Especially not vegetables. Mom started feeding me in my favorite place. She made it a game. I became the mouse, not Joanie anymore. The mouse was hungry. Hungry enough to eat the Policano boys. Mom lifted the tablecloth and gave me one green bean at a time. First I ate Joey, then Donny, then Michael, Thomas, Louie and Andrew. In no time, the beans disappeared. I knew we were pretending. I wasn't really eating Louie and his brothers. But I never told Louie. I didn't want him to be afraid to come over.

On Sundays when we had nothing planned, I climbed into the trolley and went to church with Louie and his family. My parents didn't mind, though we were Jewish. What did they do while I was gone?

One afternoon Mom and I went to see Dr. Bokker. He smiled a lot. It moved his mustache up and down.

"Your mother's going to have a baby. Do you want a brother or sister?"

That was a surprise. No one told me. How did he know?

"A brother. If it's a sister, I'll flush her down the toilet."

"Joanie, don't talk like that," Mom said.

"I mean it. I want a brother. Louie's lucky. He has five."

"Don't worry, Mrs. Seliger," Dr. Bokker said. "I like girls. Can I keep her?"

I saw him wink his right eye at Mom.

"Thanks, Dr. Bokker. I'll talk it over with my husband."

I saw her wink her right eye back.

I liked Dr. Bokker.

Whenever possible, I sat on my *tushie* under the table. I needed to hear about my cousins. Aunt Luba always complained about Howie. Five years older and in fourth grade, he was Trouble. Just yesterday she sent him outside in his clean pants and shirt to wait while she dressed to visit Aunt Minka.

"Ten minutes I took," Luba said. "I went downstairs and there he was, fighting with Michael Policano, his shirt ripped and bloody, his pants dipped in mud. I smacked him so hard in the head, my hand hurt."

"You shouldn't hit him in the head," Mom said. "It could damage his brain."

"You're right, Fanka. Abie says the same. But Howie makes me so mad, I can't help myself."

Cousin Ruthie was a different story. A freshman at Midwood High, she got up early to brush her hair a hundred strokes, she told me, and to pick the right pleated skirt and sweater set.

"It's important to dress right when you're in high school. You never know which boy will notice."

Aunt Luba complained Ruthie was "boy-crazy." All she talked about was Eddie or Donny or Andrew.

I liked Eddie best. Once he borrowed his father's car.

"I don't want you alone in the car with that boy," Aunt Luba said. "If you go, you have to take Joanie."

"What do you think I'll do?" Ruthie yelled, "that I need a five-year-old to keep an eye on me?"

From under the table, I could tell she was mad.

"Ruchela, calm down," Aunt Luba said. "I had boyfriends. I know where kisses can go."

What was she talking about? Kisses went on cheeks.

"Stop it, Ma! It's broad daylight. Eddie wants to take me for a ride."

"If you go, Joanie goes. Fanka can use a nap."

"I am tired," I heard Mom say. "The baby kicks and wakes me up."

Where was Mom hiding the baby? It must be a girl. Was she afraid to let me see her? Did she think I'd really flush her down the toilet? Would I? Maybe Ruthie knew what was going on. In the car, I'd ask.

Ruthie put me in the back seat. She sat up front, squeezed close to Eddie. It was fun to look out the window. We passed Rosenthal's Grocery. We passed my schoolyard where we lined up for recess. The playground where I pumped my legs to swing high. Eddie kept driving. We passed houses and stores I didn't recognize. He and Ruthie talked about a school dance. I think they forgot I was there. That didn't matter. I felt happy to be in the car, to ride anywhere.

Eddie drove into a tunnel. All of a sudden it went dark. Water started splashing against the windows. Arms came out from the walls. A monster was pushing the car. Would he open my door and pull me out? Squeeze me till I couldn't breathe? I started screaming.

"It's only a car wash," Ruthie said. "Stop screaming."

I couldn't stop. Eddie never took me for another ride. When they broke up at the dance, Ruthie blamed me.

"I'll never take you anywhere," she said. "You spoiled everything with your stupid screaming."

I missed Eddie and wished Ruthie weren't mad at me.

After morning kindergarten, I liked to explore the room she shared with Howie. There were two skinny beds on opposite walls. With chalk, Ruthie drew a white line on the floor to divide the room. Any time Howie crossed to her side, she pushed him back. If he rubbed out the line, she smacked him.

"It's bad enough having to share," she told me. "Much worse with a bratty brother."

Ruthie had a dresser with a mirror. My favorite pastime was to open Ruthie's top drawer, take out her pastel satin ribbons–each so carefully ironed, spooled and clamped with a bobby pin–and try them on, one after another.

They were all so beautiful. I never could decide which color I liked best. One day I'd choose blue, the next green. Then pink or red. Ruthie said you should match your ribbon to your blouse or skirt or sweater.

In between ribbons, I brushed my blonde curls with Ruthie's brush. I liked the soft white bristles. They didn't hurt the way Mom's black bristles did when she brushed hard to untangle my knots. With a brush like Ruthie's, I could brush a hundred strokes. I could make my hair shine, too.

I wished Ruthie were my sister. That the other skinny bed was mine, not Howie's. Maybe Mom and Dad could come live here with me and Ruthie. Maybe Aunt Luba and Uncle Abie could take Howie to live in our apartment on the second floor. Even though it's smaller, they might like it better than this one on the fourth floor. Aunt Luba complained a lot, "It's not easy *shlepping* groceries up so many flights."

"Change is good," I heard Mom say when I was under the table. Was that what she meant?

A door slammed. I looked in the mirror. Ruthie.

"What do you think you're doing? I'll teach you not to touch my stuff."

"I'm sor-r-r-y," I stammered. "I'll put your ribbons away." I began to carefully roll the red one but Ruthie pulled it out of my hands.

"Shut up! I'll wash your fresh mouth out." She grabbed a cake of Lifebuoy soap from the bathroom, and yanked my mouth open. Before I could yell "Help," Ruthie shoved in the soap. With one hand on my head and the other on my chin, she pushed my mouth closed. My teeth dug deep into the soap.

Aunt Luba rushed into the room. *"Gott in Himmel!"* It took a long time to free my teeth and pull out the red cake of soap burning my throat. I gagged. My spit bubbled out. After, Aunt Luba made me rinse my mouth, then drink a glass of water. I ran home crying. How could Ruthie, my dream-sister, be that mean?

Mom put me to bed early. I heard her and Aunt Luba in the kitchen.

"How could my Ruthie do that to your Joanie?" Aunt Luba asked Mom. "No parties, no boys knocking at the door for a month." Mom disagreed. "Ruthie went berserk, but Joanie provoked her. You know how Ruthie loves her ribbons."

In the end, I was glad Ruthie got off with a talking-to from Uncle Abie. I didn't want her to hate me. But her temper scared me, so I stayed away from her room.

Mom took me to the Five and Ten around the block. She let me pick three ribbons: pink, green, baby blue. In the morning, I chose the pink one. Mom tied it tightly around my curls. Then she made a bow like the one Shirley Temple wore in the movies. I spooled the other two, clamped them with bobby pins, put them carefully in my drawer.

After school, I sat under the table. I untied the bow and took off the pretty pink ribbon, then smoothed it flat. I would give it to my baby sister. Mom didn't need to hide her anymore.

This is the power of gathering: it inspires us, delightfully, to be more hopeful, more joyful, more thoughtful: in a word, more alive.

Alice Waters

Contact Tracing

by LISA EVE CHEBY

from *GLOBALPOEMIC*

i.
Rain in Griffith Park and my last human contact.
I snuck out early from day-one of work-from-home.
I lay my naked body face down under the sheet.

After Marika prepared my body with oils, before I return
to begin shelter at home, the rain and no one but I
walk in Griffith Park. The eucalyptus and longleaf pines are closer
than six feet, their branches brush, alive and fearlessly fragrant.

Five men play golf as cars swish by. My umbrella still proclaims
slogans from last year's teachers' strike, where I learned
it is acceptable to walk in the rain
                    healthy   doable
                                                            even necessary.

ii.
Eight days ago, when we were still pretending
our lives could persist
unaltered, we chose
the air & space
of Descanso Gardens over
a museum. We were already washing
hands more profusely, denying
hugs. We leaned up to smell
the cherry blossom, caressed
the rough skin of trees.

Today   to feed my skin
I brush the Norfolk Island Pine

on my balcony   I had been craving
slowness, to clear the way for learning
                                        to say no,
                                                to value
time, the only yield
we can never recoup.

But now

iii.

The balcony rail steams like mountains warming in daybreak.
The plants drip accumulated dew that dampens the chair &
    my thighs.
The birds reclaim the mornings like humans their journals.

It has taken 13 days since Grace hugged me,
after the yoga class where I brought my own props,
for me to let gratitude seep in like the rain

carries in a wintery cold waking me from a fevered dream.
How should my body temperature feel on cold nights
under a down blanket?

iv.

Now is the crying stage, even for the introverts.
This is not Christmas or a retreat.
Someone is making bacon and I am alone.

Pandemic Post

by HAZEL KIGHT WITHAM and NORIKO NAKADA

These poem-missives were exchanged across the summer and fall of 2020. They were inspired by "Envelopes of Air," a series of poems by Ada Limón and Natalie Diaz published in The New Yorker *in the spring of 2018. They were one small way these writer/teacher/mothers stayed connected through a global pandemic.*

final friday of summer

hkw to nakada

I woke this morning in my home for the first time in days

the desert was prickly relief within cactus of dread
on last Monday before school year
the small griefs of travel seeping up from sticky carpet
111 degree heat panting midday, keeping us cloistered, screened

I am noticing all the things I find to begrudge,
how usually what breaks me is the run, sweat loosens the locks,
uncages brain
I've been doing so much teacher-time these days, Nori
even while on air-quote break

This morning you and I write together, apart
and the last image I have of you
is your son head-bopping your chin
how the exuberance of five often equals oops and ow

boundaries are slippery now, all screen-tethered and to-do list
echo of connection comes through prison portals.
I am remembering the long hours of companied leisure,
the storied wilderness we wandered,

not flash image that cuts to mute vanish.

At night, in the desert, while kids were screen-rapt
D and R and I drifted weightless in the aqua of pool glow,
scooped praying mantis from siren-song of beckoning water
wandered through stories of our past selves, those people who
    knew nothing of now

I'm going to work on gratitude again,
and thanks to Ross Gay, delight
I'm going to work on patience and small daily practice
seeing big things through to satisfying end

I'm still anxious about the stone sorrow I am trying to tell,
but now, from you, I have a spider web jasper gemstone,
to filter out the worry
and keep unspooling the story

There is something to the breathtaking urgency of now,
letting go of all that did not serve
rescuing ourselves from the frantic chop,
drenched but alive, offering prayer into the clutched air

relishing this new view.

can we talk about the weather?

nakada to hkw

Can we talk a little bit more about the desert
about the air and the pools of conversation
our past lives floating
because we are trapped and the rest feels so disparate, so far away?

Can we talk about the praying mantis
rescued from a watery grave
and the praying it might have done
but probably didn't, still resulting in its resurrection?

Can we talk less about teaching
and more about writing
although the two are so linked
we can never seem to have one conversation without the other.

I forgot to tell you I recorded a reading
I'll never use.
It captures the lyrics of REM's "Hairshirt"
and an excerpt of "Drive." *You are beautiful. This life.*

Let's click a cassette tape into a car stereo and drive away
even if just for a few moments
and escape these prison portals
these voices calling out to us from every corner of this gentle trap.

What would you listen to, Haze?
Could we breathe sitting next to one another
with the windows down
and let go of the fear that we might be killing one another?

Can we talk about how beautiful it all is
and how fucked up? I know, we must find a way
to keep breathing when even these envelopes,
these words, these missives fail to fill the void.

lowest rung

hkw to nakada

I'm soaking now in your high school songs—
listening to the pummel of "Drive"
dreaming of the next road trip where we run from our lives
someday when we've decided to map a way through risk.

Funny, I've never listened to "Hairshirt"—
but I like the idea of hanging wrong on the lowest rung
even as I understand the twisted draw to ruin ourselves
before someone else can.

I got the news late as always
this time from small boy who spied
big horror on the largest
screen we own.

He kept repeating the details—
7 shots in the back, he was Black, running for his life
the questions—Why? What color were the police?
and this—Did his children cry?

I have no answers, only more questions.

Instead, I sift through day to pull small seam of delight:
even without classroom,
a student lingered on screen to ask after book
is there any greater gift than this work

of stitching our lives together, delicate webs
of books and brokenness, words and songs
we sing across snarl of distance
this unmapped marathon to uncertain finish line.

I want to risk us away to writing retreat,
a small inhale of smokeless life,

while West Coast edges burn
and everything begs for relief.

I want to say I'll lockdown and test and be safe to do so
so the air we share is clear and free,
for a small space where we can hang our fears
on the lowest rung.

Nori, it feels we are squandering our lives
I want our children to play together again,
but what can we promise anyone anymore?
I have no answers, only more questions.

What could we do if we decided to
rethink threat, let running man go
repent this broken history, reckon with our past
and breathe together in the landscape of unknowns?

Which is, of course, where we have always been,
even when we told ourselves otherwise.

such a time (more of the same)

nakada to hkw

When the grief of this life has worn me too worried
when day-I-can't-keep-track bleeds into another of the same
I wonder what laying down these burdens might look like.

What is it to quit?
I have been told we cannot do such things
but I'm ready to lay it all down.

To lift bones from bed feels burdensome.
To wrestle children from sleep
knowing and not knowing what the day will hold
is both light and exhaustion.

It's more of the same, Haze.
It's leaving me in a familiar/unfamiliar state.

Take it in gulps
the air
the news
the risks
the ash
the heartache
the teaching
the questions
the fire
the parenting
the writing
the reading

all-consuming

discerning answers

seeking hope

knowing tomorrow

the morning bleeds
into more of the same.

It is too much.
It is all that remains.

good place to start

hkw to nakada

It's been weeks now since I've poemed across these miles.
Tonight I am raw girl, father-fearing
in this time of hugless and lonely
solo room, long days

I'm still working on gratitude,
and I do not have my own map
only borrowed ones, worn soft
I keep rereading to compass my way forward

My father is somewhere on that island,
neither of us reaching out, and the broken of us
is something I imagine will lift with loss
maybe I am the one forgetting

What am I doing
to be the person I want to be
but looking to others to guide me,
then pretending I might know a way.

I miss you, friend.
I miss brussels sprouts, yellowtail, caramel budino
the grounding from writer-sister
who is so much braver than I.

Tomorrow I'll text invite to small birthday gather
for boy who is growing into nine
and I know the answer will likely be no
and I will tell myself I won't take it personally

not in times like these
and we'll keep doing the screen thing
but I am atrophying in this pixelated facsimile
I just keep hoping we survive.

The systems are failing us, are failing our students,
and I do not know how to better any of it,
but to work on listening, be okay with good-ish
to let go of my need to please, to save, to heal.

George Floyd's birthday is coming, so is an election
I need to listen to what Patricia Smith told us today:
look for the beauty where everything is ugly
look for the humor when there is nothing funny

and I think that is a good place to start
there's so much material, isn't there?

a false choice

nakada to hkw

I woke up the other morning
with the first lines of this poem on my heart

Is it safe yet
to celebrate?

Your last poem reminded me of levity,
a good place to start.

But that was before the election and the most recent surge
before doctors and nurses urged us all again

not to look away.

Still, I remind myself that
I need the light and laughter.

Seeing how bad and serious
has never been my problem.

So I write again because the words still show up here
despite doubt and neglect.

because my body keeps carrying me through these days
although I curse and critique it and do not let it rest.

because time outdoors has done me good
and our planet still sustains us despite our abuse.

because blood is blue until you are cut wide open, exposing red
and the purple bruise of our country might start to heal

Yes, it's a good place to start.

What other choice do we have?

To not begin?

Under congested incandescence of
pulsing city
the world bends itself into a village.
Here: our great gathering place.

Amanda Gorman

EMERGENCY

by GERDA GOVINE ITUARTE

Nursing
Home
Petri
dish

germs
circulate
four
beds

in
room
noisy
supplies

snatch
lives
disconnected
confused

world
spinning
normal
on

life
support
unknown
territory

vaccines
approved
delivery
system

broken
demand
high
supply

low
patients
nurses
doctors

waiting
game
intense
on

hold
business
as usual
reality

first
will
be
first

equipment
shortage
unprepared
residents

families
not
allowed
to see

each
other
death
enters

mask
wash
hands
best

options
six
feet
apart

six
feet
under
two

weary
inequity
grows
severe

cannot
hide
behind
mask

numbers
tell
story
again

last
will
be
last

worry
no
answers
stuck

mercy
cries
emergency
emergency

From Inside a Burning Building

by ROMAINE WASHINGTON

from *PURGATORY HAS AN ADDRESS*

i am writing from inside a burning building.
the cell phone in the corner keeps asking,
how am i doing? what do i see?
does it hurt as bad as it smells?

i have lost my sense of smell,
but understand
we must document these things
because we are here and still alive.

my hair is charcoal.
skin is peeling layers of tears.
scientists say the skin weeps
when it is badly burned.

the air tastes like tires
though i have never tasted a tire,
this is how i imagine it tastes.

this is what i must tell the cell phone
so, it has a simile to understand,

there are really no words to describe
how it feels to be inside a burning building.

there are no words to capture,
the sensation of walls eating you alive.

i look at windows exploding
knowing they will be there tomorrow,
the same time,
ready to explode again.

my cell phone rings,
Covid is calling from a hospital bed.

i cannot visit my friend
whose fever is so high
she is hallucinating.

she says:
i am sweat
pouring from my eyes,
yelling at me,
"there are stories to be written."

she says,
i am sorry,
but i can't.

she hangs up the phone.
tomorrow she is telling me
it feels good to be quarantined
where the sheets are white,
and the quiet is eating me alive.

Women of Dogwood

by TISHA MARIE REICHLE-AGUILERA

CHARACTERS

EQUIS, elder, descendant of the Kumeyaay people, neither alive nor dead but exists simultaneously in this world and the next.

TIERRA, 27-year-old farmer, skin the color of the earth, daughter of Mexican woman.

SORA, late twenties also, Tierra's best friend and neighbor, Japanese American teacher.

TIME AND PLACE

2045 Imperial Valley, California–part of Sonora Desert

SETTING

A dirt road between two fields. North Dogwood Road and South Dogwood Road signs are prominent at each end. The Colorado River is to the left of the fields, the natural separation between the Imperial Valley and Arizona. Trailers along the Arizona side.

SCENE ONE

Field in full sun in front of a vast expanse of desert. Dark and cloudy in the distance.

TIERRA squats next to a field and scoops up a handful of soil. She watches it pass from one hand to the other several times-

Rubs grains between her fingers. Tastes it. Freezes in place.

EQUIS

Offstage–recites the legend (borrowed from Pat Mora) in rhythm with the action below.

El desierto es tu madre.
Le digo, abrázame
Me susurra, "Acuéstate aqui."
Le digo cántame.
Me arrulla con sus canciones de viento.
Le digo enséñame
Y florece en el brillo del sol, en el silencio de la nieve, en las arenas más secas.
El desierto es tu madre.

In the distance, near the South Dogwood Road sign, a MEXICAN WOMAN holds a swaddled baby tight to her chest, slips through a break in the fence. She looks around, desperate for a hiding place in the desert. At the base of two Pacific Dogwood trees, she sits in the shade and feeds the infant the last of her breaks milk. She digs a shallow space where she sat and places the sleeping baby there. She runs about, gathering large flat stones and places them around the child for protection. She exits as the fence is removed. A woodpecker appears in the tree. A coyote lays its head on its paws and keeps watch over the sleeping infant.

TIERRA gets up and moves along the furrow, pulling weeds, inspecting the stalks. The light follows her as she wanders to the Pacific Dogwood trees at the end of the road and walks around them, scans the desert. Feeds coyote a piece of jerky from her pocket.

Woodpecker noise.

SCENE TWO

Continuous

EQUIS holds burlap bag and walks to front edge of same corn field. Watches TIERRA walk off as the sun sets. EQUIS stands in the moonlight.

SORA joins her with a plastic bag full of frozen fish heads.

SORA

I left Tierra a message that I'd be out with other teachers tonight so she's on her own for dinner.

EQUIS

She'll believe that? Of course. She wouldn't go even if you invited her.

SORA

She never wants to go anywhere with anyone.

EQUIS

Kind of hoped she'd outgrow that.

SORA

She's 27. Shouldn't it have happened already?

EQUIS

Her mother didn't live to 27, so we can't know what she'll be like.

SORA

And her dad?

EQUIS

He was still breathing last I checked. But she doesn't need to know that.

SORA

Doesn't need to know.

Beat.

I brought these like you asked. But why can't Tierra know?

EQUIS

She thinks my methods are old-fashioned. She has been resistant to the old ways recently. I worry I'm losing her.

EQUIS walks across the road to the empty field. Her cane ends in a post hole digger operated by a button on top she presses with her thumb.

SORA drops a fish head in each hole.

EQUIS drops three seeds, murmurs a prayer, and pushes the earth back over the seeds with her foot. She takes three strides up the field and digs the next hole.

They repeat this process, heading South toward the Dogwood trees as they continue talking.

SORA

She's not going anywhere. She hates that I still go to "enemy territory" to fish. Refuses to believe some San Diegans aren't out to get us.

EQUIS

There's reason to believe they want this region. And she is determined that will never happen.

SORA

Not you too! Been reading the conspiracy papers?

EQUIS

(chuckles) I don't have to. I know what happened here before the walls and fences were built. Before they came down. What still happens beyond our region now.

SORA

Isn't a lot of it feminist propaganda?

EQUIS

It has its merits. Some truths. There's a reason patriarchy was destroyed. Why we work so hard to preserve our matrilineal traditions here.

SORA

It is more peaceful here.

COYOTE howls.

EQUIS

And we plan to keep it that way. Do whatever it takes.

SORA

All the elders agree? Even the men?

EQUIS

Especially the men. They are just as tormented by the memories of restrictions and violence as the rest of us. Many of them gave up. Went to el otro lado and stayed.

SORA

Do you think about it? Finally resting?

EQUIS

Too much to do here. Can't leave Tierra until she's... Not yet. She's not ready yet.

EQUIS kneels at the base of the two Dogwood trees and sifts through the earth there.
COYOTE joins her. She scoops handfuls into her bag.

Woodpecker noise.

SORA picks fruit from the twin Dogwood trees and puts them into a clean bag.

They walk back along the path of the planted seeds, EQUIS drizzles a thick line of the sandy soil across the top of them.

SORA

(points at the line of freshly turned earth) How long before they'll break surface?

EQUIS

Less than a week. They'll be the same height as those in a few weeks. More abundant at harvest.

SORA

She gets mad when you do things like this. She may not say it to you out of respect, but –

EQUIS

But I know. I always know.

Beat.

She needs to see. She won't listen so she has to be shown.

SORA

A few things I should show her.

EQUIS

You don't need to confront her. Not yet. Your relationship is too new.

SORA

New? We've been friends since second grade. Almost 20 years.

EQUIS

And you want to stay friends for even more. So not long if you're looking at a lifetime.

SORA

True. But do I really want that? She's so difficult sometimes. More frequently the past seven years.

EQUIS

Because she's figuring out who she really is and how different you two are.

SORA

I don't know how we can be. We've both been here this whole time.

EQUIS

But you weren't born here. Not of this earth. You carry memories of different people, of a different place.

SORA

I don't remember before here. I was four when my grandparents brought me. My only memories of my parents are the stories they've told me, the photographs I saved from the fire.

EQUIS

Do you want to remember more?

SORA

You can do that?

EQUIS

No. But I know elders who can.

SORA

Elders here? Did they know my grandparents?

EQUIS

They followed them here. For safety. It is possible they knew your parents too.

SORA

Who? Why don't I know them?

EQUIS

They spend most of their time al otro lado.

SORA

But you can ask them to return?

EQUIS

If that's what you want.

Beat.

But really think about why you want the memories. Sometimes our pasts aren't pleasant to revisit. There's a reason memories fade.

SORA exits.

EQUIS walks to river for her nightly bath.

SCENE THREE

Sunrise.

TIERRA walks to SORA's front porch with two mugs, humming a song.

SORA

You're rather pleasant this morning.

TIERRA

I slept without interruption.

SORA hands TIERRA the bag full of dogwood berries.

TIERRA trades for the mug.

TIERRA

Smell that?

SORA looks in bag and smells.

TIERRA

Not the bag. The wind.

Trees are still. Nothing in nature moves.

SORA

(sips from mug) What wind? All I smell is this.

TIERRA

I put canela like you like.

SORA

You don't like?

TIERRA

Tea. Coffee makes me too awake. I can't hear or smell right.

SORA

What did you smell?

TIERRA

The Sea. It's clean again. Salinity levels back to normal. Healthy water. Soon we'll be able to raise our own fish there.

SORA

The elders won't eat them. Their memory of the Salton Sea is corrupt.

TIERRA

There was a time it wasn't. Equis can remind them. I've read about its recreational use.

SORA

What kind of fish?

TIERRA

The Salton Sea used to be full of sargo, orange mouth corvina, and croaker. We'll start with tilapia. They are a hardier species. Like the warm water. We want to try bluefin tuna, too, but we'll have to separate the two.

SORA

How?

TIERRA

Divide the sea. Secondary engineering students are building a structure now out of last year's corn harvest waste.

SORA

Thank you, Moses.

TIERRA

The secondary students are growing algae and other plants for fish food in the tanks outside the warehouse. They've made them resistant to the bacteria that plagues the lake in the 1970s. Figured out how to regulate their oxygen use too. No more toxins from mega farms.

SORA

We have amazing students here, don't we?

TIERRA

They have an amazing teacher.

SORA

It's not just me. You've taught them a lot too.

TIERRA

They also have plans to use the fish waste for fertilizer. And they detoxified the old fish bones found in the sand so we can use them for compost.

Beat.

By next year, you won't have to go fishing in San Diego anymore.

SORA

(tone not as supportive as her words) Total sustainability. That's our goal.

Beat.

What about birds?

TIERRA

There are sonic devices that keep birds away from the water's surface. But we haven't had brown pelicans here since...

SORA

Since we had fish. Before my time. You should ask Equis.

TIERRA

I'm sure secondary students know.

(sips tea) Don't want to make you late for work.

(lifts bag) Going to smash these for salad dressing. Dinner?

SORA

Tonight? Sure.

TIERRA walks back toward her house.

SORA

Tierra?

TIERRA

Yes?

SORA

You're welcome.

TIERRA

(sings) Thank you, because you didn't have to. Thank you with everything I am.

SORA

(groans) You have to stop listening to the oldies.

TIERRA

All the other stations are staticky. I need to have someone check my service.

SORA, with a guilty face, watches TIERRA walk home.

SCENE FOUR

Darkness. TIERRA's bedroom window.

Loud noises outside.

TIERRA

What the hell?

EQUIS

I need your long-handled hoe.

TIERRA

Right now? It's the middle of the night.

EQUIS

End. Not middle. Almost time for my river bath.

TIERRA

It's still dark enough to see all the stars. Why hoe? Why now?

EQUIS

Last quarter. Tilling the earth with as little light as possible prevents weeds from growing. Or at least prevents so many.

TIERRA

The earth is fine. Let it rest. Let me rest. (rolls over)

EQUIS

It could be better.

TIERRA

What are you tilling for anyway?

EQUIS

You could learn the old ways too.

TIERRA

Can I learn them in the morning?

EQUIS

There will be too much sun in the morning.

TIERRA

That's what I mean. I need sunlight to see.

EQUIS

So do the weeds.

TIERRA

You're not going to leave, are you?

EQUIS

I will if you tell me where the hoe is.

TIERRA

Let me get shoes on. Might as well learn something now that I'm up. I can help you hoe.

EQUIS

Don't need help. Just the hoe.

TIERRA

What was all that noise?

EQUIS

Your shed is a mess.

TIERRA

It wasn't before you went in there.

EQUIS

Why do you move things? How can you find them in the dark?

TIERRA

Normal people don't go digging around there in the dark. (goes outside)

EQUIS

They do if they want to till away the possibility of weeds.

TIERRA

Why are you so afraid of weeds?

EQUIS

Not afraid of anything. Some weeds are medicinal. But I don't want them choking my tomatillos.

TIERRA

Tomatoes? (she stops before handing over the hoe) It's too early for tomato planting.

EQUIS

It's an experiment. Seeds I saved.

TIERRA

When?

EQUIS

From el otro lado.

TIERRA

Great. Death seeds.

EQUIS

Seeds give life.

TIERRA

What's wrong with the tomato seeds I have?

EQUIS

Nothing. These are different. Tomatillo.

TIERRA

How?

EQUIS

They're more firm, not as juicy, tart, and green.

TIERRA

Green? Who ever heard of green tomatoes? No one wants to eat green tomatoes.

EQUIS

Toma*tillos*. We used to. All our gente used to. But when you were very young and the government was at its most corrupt, the borders at their most volatile, they were banned from este lado. Along with serrano chiles, cilantro, cebollitas, and aguacate. All the good stuff.

TIERRA

I've been farming this land almost 15 years. Why am I just hearing about this now?

EQUIS

It wasn't safe when you started. We had to be careful what we brought over until the walls and fences were all gone. Until those who feared and loathed us were gone.

TIERRA

So at least the last seven years?

EQUIS

I tried to mention it once. You wouldn't listen. Dismissed my traditional ways. Thought you knew everything.

TIERRA

Was I asleep when you mentioned all those lost crops?

TIERRA starts hoeing the patch of earth outside her bedroom window, a small garden.

TIERRA

It's a lot harder to hear when I'm asleep. Maybe instead of sneaking into my subconscious while I'm asleep or waking me up before dawn to hoe, you could actually stop by during the day. Knock on the door, say, Hey, Tierra, I've got some ancient farming wisdom to share.

EQUIS follows behind TIERRA on her hands and knees, takes tiny plants out of her pockets, pokes a hole in the earth with her finger, and gently places the seedling into the hole. She holds her hands around each root and murmurs a prayer.

TIERRA continues hoeing the square of earth, wiping sweat, mumbling about these new plants.

El Norte

by DINAH BERLAND

from *HOTEL AT THE END OF THE WORLD*

When border police lift children from
their mothers' arms, their fathers' hands—
lock them up in cages from El Paso
to El Monte—tossing silver sheets
across small bodies, toddlers cry so hard
they can hardly catch their breath.
Meanwhile agents shuttle parents
onto airplanes like so much cargo,
shipping them to jail in Topeka, Chicago,
after they had walked for weeks
with feet on fire toward El Norte—
the land that was supposed to save them.

When a deported Guatemalan mother
hides her head in her hands, afraid
she will never see her only child again—
Graciela, age seven, who had just learned
to play Mozart on her three-quarter-size violin—
I wonder how my grandparents felt
as they rushed to escape the Czar's army,
descending by nightfall into the cavernous
belly of a ship, tossing for days
on unknown waters. How did it feel
to step off the boat at Ellis Island?
Did Grandpa hoist little Aunt Fanny
to his shoulders, so she could see
the lady holding her lamp high?
Did tears arise in Grandma's eyes,
her belly big with Aunt Sophia,
the one who would become a violinist?

When the US attorney general poses
before TV cameras, smirking as he spouts

chapter and verse to justify ripping
families apart, I think of Thailand
where twelve soccer players—boys
who had never learned to swim—
huddle together deep inside a cave
accessible only by serpentine tunnels, now
flooded. Their coach, a Buddhist monk,
teaches them to meditate so they can
endure the wait. Meanwhile
divers in wetsuits gear up with
scuba tanks and masks—two men
for each boy: one to cradle a child beneath
his body, the other to follow a guide rope
through the tunnel. We follow them
each morning in the news until two by two,
then four, then eight—all the boys,
their coach and guides, are borne
by unseen hands into silver sheets of light.

What If They Told You

by CYNTHIA ALESSANDRA BRIANO

from *OURSTORY*

The Bracero Program, you called it, and I
held up my hands before your officers,

waited for their nod at my nails, eroded and bold
with dirt, the creases lined black like a sketch

of a hand instead of a hand, proof I was broken
in, so you clapped and shooed me into a wooden
crate, the back of a truck tall with beams

like a fence that encloses el ganado, the winnings, the game,
covered our peripheral vision, and we were driven.

You invited me here during that war, needed me
to replace the man you had sent away to die.
What if they told you your hands were born rough with the
promise

of toil, that callus and cuts are credentials
inspected before you were allowed

to hunch down and rip out even the root,
strain upward and tear off even the stem,

strap the harness of a double-sacked burlap
over your chest and back, weigh it down good.

The prize goes to the one who can fill up the most
crates in an hour, work faster than the man beside you,

Let's see—a race—who is the best?

I knew the man who worked beside me,
the man who was never taught to read,

the one who was told to sign
for his pay with a print of the finger.

I wasn't always around to count the hours
unaccounted for on his end of the month

winnings. I wasn't around to say his name
before his heat-stricken body was sent off, crate

tagged with the grower's best guess
of a number. My grandfather

says men who were never taught to read
were told to sign for their pay with a print of a finger.

Give us another digit, this one's too faint to tell.

Sometimes only the small, digits on the left hand
had grooves enough to count. Easily, after much,

they wear away. The only thing
my grandfather knew how to write was his name.

My bed becomes a cot at night, and I look down
with eyes buried narrow and faint, slit
under raw scorch of sun, down at the fields

neatly combed in rows on my fingertips,
I swallow hard at the dry, memory of thirst,

try to find the end, or even the beginning
of these familiar curves and find

only splintered stories. The proof
has split in half at the sore,

split like a rock down the sand-
yellow center and I could

barely make out my own mark.
The lines have chafed away and sunken

into the flat, faceless soil
of my hardened brown skin.

mutual aid

by ELIZABETH GALOOZIS

for Caro

we will make a place in the desert for us.
for the gray survivors
of every kind of violence,
natural or human.
there,
we will find
and tend
wellsprings, resilient plants.
grow out our wild hair
or cut it all off.
listen to
and say
whatever we want,
including
nothing.
make a table
we all want to eat from.
make dark rooms
to rest in the peak of the sun.
leach out the residues,
the microparticles of pollution,
of our former lives
from our blood and breath.
hold each other's hands
and say,
we're
here
now.

The Distance Between

by NICOLE ZIMMERMAN

from *MASON STREET REVIEW*

I awaken to dawn light illuminating the glossy privet, its white clusters of fragrant blossoms attracting honey bees to its branches. Their distant buzzing drifts through the open window as I slip back into drowsy sleep. Most mornings, still in my robe, I sip coffee on the side porch while the sun warms my back. Make bed. Wash face. Open the farm gate. Cow parsnip unfurls its white frill for goldfinches to perch, not far from the bearded iris—its petals on display like a ruffled tuxedo ready for a party. The first poppy marked the spring equinox, a passage that nearly went unnoticed during our first week of shelter-in-place.

Each day is laced with an overlay of anxiety: the plummeting economy; the projection that fifty-five percent of Californians will become infected; the shortages on grocery store shelves. At the start of our statewide lockdown, I went shopping and stared at a wall of vacant glass where the greens should be. The paper aisle had nothing left but Kleenex: two boxes per customer allowed. I filled my shopping cart with a couple weeks' worth of provisions plus a surplus of cleaning supplies and health remedies for the long haul, in case one of us gets sick. We're doing our part to protect the community, I justified. The more infrequent our outings, the less contact, the better. Seven containers of hazelnut milk admittedly constituted a panic buy.

While I waited behind the six-foot demarcation, an elderly woman in front of me carried just the basics in her basket—bread, milk, bananas. She coughed multiple times into her hand, then grabbed at a plastic bag floating to the linoleum floor.

"She's not sanitizing," I warned another customer who considered the line. He wore a protective face covering before it was ubiquitous, but pivoted away.

"Some people just don't get it," I complained to the checkout clerk, who ignored my commentary while unloading my cart along the same conveyor belt. My mind obsessed over disinfecting everything with Clorox wipes later. Yet in the rising silence my face reddened. In the absence of collusion, I felt remorse. I had reacted from fear for my own safety, but what about showing concern for hers? Maybe the woman was ill, living alone, getting by on a limited income. Could she secure enough food? I thought about my ninety-seven-year-old great aunt in Virginia, the youngest of eleven siblings and the longest to live, with arthritic hands but a sharp mind, who required daily caregivers yet could no longer touch loved ones. What about all the people trapped in convalescent homes, incarcerated, or held in detention facilities at the border? How did the hundreds of thousands across American cities who remained unhoused cope during stay-at-home orders? I realized that in my quickness to judge, I had distanced myself from my own humanity.

In the afternoon my wife and I dig compost into garden beds, prepping them to grow lettuces, beans, eggplants, and tomatoes purchased from a nursery down the road—still considered essential. With the fresh produce we'll make sauces and homemade soups, storing the mason jars in the chest freezer alongside packs of pasture-raised lamb. Amid this bucolic scene, with acres of sheep fields fencing us in from our neighbors, it's easy to lose sight of others. Certainly we count ourselves among the fortunate.

Come summer we'll welcome a parade of visitors to the pool, everyone maintaining the requisite distance. In late autumn we will rent an Airbnb outside Joshua Tree National Park, stopping for lunch with my cousin and his husband on their outdoor patio in Palm Springs. A few days later one of them contracts a fever with severe migraines, testing positive for the coronavirus, followed by the other within ten days. Both survive without joining some 93,000 hospitalized patients—an all-time high in the United States—among the one and a half million cases then confirmed worldwide. My great aunt, too, will become ill from COVID, transmitted by a caregiver. After two weeks in the ICU she spends her birthday on the beach, happily eating an ice cream from her wheelchair on a boardwalk. Some months later, in early winter, her lungs will fill with fluid and she'll pass away at home, joining the ancestors while her children are unable to come to her side to say goodbye.

By the time the first poppy marks another spring equinox, my wife and I are vaccinated against the virus and possibly its variants, along with nearly one-third of the nation. I awaken to dawn light illuminating the glossy privet, its white clusters of fragrant blossoms attracting honey bees to its branches. Their distant buzzing drifts through the open window as I awaken. I sip coffee on the side porch while the sun warms my back. Make bed. Wash face. Open the farm gate. Cow parsnip unfurls its white frill for goldfinches to perch, not far from the bearded iris—its petals on display like a ruffled tuxedo ready for a party. Tree swallows swarm from their nests, their sharp-edged wings like paper airplanes, their iridescent blue-green feathers shimmering. A collective hum fills the air as they net the sky of insects.

May we honor other people's feelings
respect their anger, sadness, grief,
joy as we do our own.
Though we tremble before uncertain futures
may we meet illness, death,
and adversity with strength
may we dance in the face of
our fears.

Gloria Anzaldúa

How I Respond to a Health Care Survey

by ALIXEN PHAM

after Solmaz Sharif

IN THE LAST SIX MONTHS how often have you seen your

PROVIDER? The one who charges me $300 for

CHECK-UP and SPECIALIZED CARE about my health, but never

ADVICE about what to do when my mother was dying. Instead asking:

HOW MANY DAYS DID YOU USUALLY HAVE TO WAIT for her body to shut down?

MEDICAL QUESTIONS needed to be asked

DURING REGULAR OFFICE HOURS as I waited in darkness for the sun's

FOLLOW UP to give me death's time table. Would it squeeze my mother in:

SAME DAY
1 DAY
2-3 DAYS
4-7 DAYS
8-14 DAYS
15-30 DAYS
MORE THAN 30 DAYS. At which point, who do I call? Who would

EXPLAIN THINGS IN A WAY THAT WAS EASY TO UNDERSTAND? Who would

LISTEN CAREFULLY TO me cry, *Don't go, I'm sorry,* even as the

BLOOD TEST, X-RAY OR OTHER TEST alerted the machines to order the casket.

CUSTOMER SERVICE STAFF gave me End-of-Care forms to sign, as if giving

WORST POSSIBLE – BEST POSSIBLE ratings about ways to die from, or survive the trauma of losing limbs, hair and organs, or loved ones could be reduced into sensible ways to

MANAGE YOUR CARE the way my mother used to manage her kitchen, treating knives, meats and vegetables with

COURTESY AND RESPECT. The neighbors and entire church praised her fried eggrolls, fried rice and shrimp & cabbage salad. Never noticed me cooking by her side. Mom's mini-me. I realized years later, she was my Institute Le Cordon Bleu, the Michelin in my star.

HOW WOULD YOU RATE YOUR OVERALL MENTAL OR EMOTIONAL HEALTH during this time? The choices are:

EXCELLENT
VERY GOOD
GOOD
FAIR
POOR—which surely can't be the lowest option, considering death is obviously worse than poor. Where are their Bedside Manners? Didn't they learn Level 101 in school? Instead, they ask me:

WHAT IS THE HIGHEST GRADE OR LEVEL OF EDUCATION THAT YOU HAVE COMPLETED? As if heaven is partitioned by high school, college, some college, graduate, PhD or Other degrees. How did anyone get in pre-language? Pre-civilizations? Pre-everything?

WHAT IS YOUR RACE (MARK ONE OR MORE), as if skin color was a factor in doling out empathy and morphine. It seemed they had failed to grasp the compassion of death when it asked:

DID SOMEONE HELP YOU COMPLETE your mother's dying?

YES, I ended her suffering. Turned off her oxygen. Upped her painkiller. Watched her last breath take *I love you* beyond my reach.

naked as a lightning rod he waited*

by LOIS P. JONES

from *ONE*

for G.W.

until everyone had left the room
and his unheld hand lay open like a question

as he passed through the pale ceiling,
rising through the hospital roof,

rising like a prize fighter from the body's defeat
to just beneath the cloud layer of Los Angeles.

He could see everything he had loved
and what had loved him and what had not.

He could see Dodger's Stadium and hear
all the cheers of games that ever were,

could catch the high fly balls
and let them fall again, those diaphanous

spheres of desire, like men who hoped
to hit something which could never be caught.

And higher across the land where
a sister walks in Descanso, past the tree

he hugged and the Mulberry with its bones
breaking out of its body, gnarled and rooted.

He could see the ducklings as they once flocked
to their feet and the fleeting conversations

rising into spring leaves. Now further up
until his beloved Pacific became a chorus line

of reclining women, like Matisse's blue nude,
the repeating waves drawing him into its perfect answer.

* *Title from a line by George Kalogeris.*

Writing Communities, Imposter Syndrome, and COVID

by CHRISTINA HOWELL

By March 2020, the entire world was holding its breath and choking back coughs. No one knew much of anything except fear and isolation. FOMO (fear of missing out) evaporated and left a puzzling hole in our lives. No one knew when we'd be able to meet in person again. For a while, we didn't even know when we'd see toilet paper on the grocery store shelves. Thankfully, I had a writing community to support and unexpectedly transform me.

In 2018, I attended my first Shut Up & Write (SUAW) meeting in Berlin with my cousin. I hovered in front of the café-meets-bookstore, imagining the well-dressed, well-educated writers inside as I tugged on my red knit dress and adjusted the peekaboo shoulders to cover my bra straps. I'd only attended one Intro to Fiction course back in junior college. I'd never been published—never even tried—plus, I was from the American Midwest. This was Berlin; surely they'd take one glance and judge me unworthy.

Densely packed bookshelves surrounded ten tiny tables that filled the small space before a simple coffee bar. The mismatched chairs were filled with people of all ages and persuasion. Some were reading, some were writing, but most were engrossed in conversation. My cousin scanned the room until she recognized someone emitting the leader vibe. She strode to his table and asked, "Is this the Shut Up & Write meetup?"

"It is." He flashed a smile, ran a hand over his prematurely white hair and gave a tug to his ponytail. He held up a finger and asked the people in his cluster to make room for two more. "Hi,

I'm Jason." He extended his hand and gestured for us to take a seat. "Welcome. Is this your first Shut Up & Write?" We nodded. "Get comfortable, get a coffee, we'll chat for fifteen minutes, then we'll start writing together."

I sat next to a cheery, white-bearded, sixty-something Irishman who told me he lived six months a year in Ireland working as an IT consultant and spent the following six writing mystery novels in Berlin.

Jason told us about his twenty-year freelance career as a writer and editor of tabletop games.

When it was my turn, I said, "Umm. I've been trying to write a memoir about my dating experiences." I blushed and avoided eye contact.

Though it was inspiring to hear of Frank and Jason's successes, it was reassuring to hear *others* introduce themselves with the words "trying to", "toying with", and "thinking about."

Fifteen minutes after the hour, Jason banged a spoon on his glass and announced, "Ok, everyone, shut up and write."

And I wrote. I wrote more in that hour than I had written in two weeks. I was half afraid someone might look over my shoulder, so I didn't dare open Facebook. There was an energy in the air, something about the tapping of fingers on keyboards and the faraway gazes that was invigorating.

After that session, I attended as many writing Meetups as I could. They asked questions I needed to hear, such as, "How many pages do you plan to write?", "What is your story arc?", "Do you have an outline?" Then they'd ask things like, "Hey, have you read *The Artist's Way*?" or "Wasn't *On Writing* by Stephen King brilliant?"

The belief that I was a "real" writer seeped into my soul after approximately 42 introductions. I no longer said, "I am trying to write a memoir," or "I am kind of writing," or "I'm not a real writer." I now introduced myself with, "Hi, I'm Christina, and I am writing a memoir."

When I moved from Berlin to Munich, I joined the local SUAW chapter and discovered Happy Writing Munich. I scheduled my classes around the writing sessions that filled my heart as well as the pages of my memoir. I loved recognizing regulars and helping new members feel welcome. Writers are a special breed. I've never experienced such a warm, supportive environment.

I recently interviewed Jessica Wright, the founder of Happy Writing, and she shared how Happy Writing got started. "Happy Writing was born in India in a little café called the London Bakery, run by a Korean family on a street with weeping willows and peacocks. It was the end of monsoon season, and gorgeous red flowers were in bloom. I wanted this happiness to spill over into my writing and bring this feeling to others. Happy Writing started online and went to in-person meetups when I moved to Munich. It's organically grown in a way that I didn't expect it to. It's become its own living, breathing organism. I love to hear people say that Happy Writing is a part of their creative process."

However, once COVID hit, in-person meetings had to be suspended. Everywhere we looked, we were getting messages to "Stay home. Save lives." Some scribbled in their journals to hold on to sanity. Some found their words had dried up. We missed meeting at cafés, but no one knew when that might again be possible, so we started meeting online.

I was stranded in England on a house sit that was supposed to last ten days but ended up stretching to thirty-six when the owners couldn't make it home. The SUAW Munich leader was stuck in Paris in his family home; in the room of his childhood, frozen in time. He couldn't face being on Zoom with his family chattering in the background, so I volunteered to take over. Reflecting on my former fears, I marveled at the ease of this transition.

One Wednesday morning, I teared up as I shared with my community that I needed to find a new place to stay, but all hotels were shut down, and all flights out of Birmingham were suspended. One writer said, "Wait, Birmingham? I know someone who has a home there, but she's stuck in Belgium. Do you want me to get in touch with her?"

A zoom call later, this stranger offered to let me stay in her home until things settled down. Little did we know that it would be four months before I could fly home to Munich.

While in England, I attended other writing groups online, sometimes up to four a day. We became part of each other's lives and creative processes. It wasn't the same as sitting next to them and sharing a private conversation, but often in a café, you couldn't hear the people on the far side of the table from you. Now, in Zoom, everyone had a voice for all to hear.

Jessica Wright shared, "I really want to highlight that what makes Happy Writing so special is not just one person behind it. It's the entire community. We have such a high level of respect for each other that no one is afraid to give their advice... Everyone has the freedom to speak up and say what they want and be the authority on a subject. It's created this organic atmosphere of trust and respect for each other's style and work. It's really special when you look at a group of people and view everyone in the room and see everyone as a core part of the community."

I met people in Nairobi, the Philippines, Spain, the United States and beyond. I loved the quilt of nationalities that the zoom squares represented. As people introduced themselves, I noticed many fellow memoirists often seemed sheepish when they shared they were working on a memoir. There's something more vulnerable about this style of writing than other genres. An idea formed. What if I could gather this group of people to inspire and support each other and motivate myself to finish my own memoir in the process?

I sent private messages to gauge interest, and 95% replied enthusiastically. So, in May 2020, I held the first Memoir Mentors Meetup. We meet every Thursday, and it has been so much more than I had ever hoped for. I can always count on this group of writers to raise my spirits when the black alligators of depression are nipping at my ankles. My life is richer, my belief in myself is stronger, and I am inspired to light this fire within others.

My name is Christina. I am an author and a leader. I inspire others to believe in themselves. I love the writing community and think you will, too. Won't you join me?

I feel that women—without wishing to foster any strict separatist notions, homo or hetero—indeed have a need for their own publications and organizations. Our problems, our experiences as women are profoundly unique as compared to the other half of the human race.

Lorraine Hansberry

Story Eater

by SABA WAHEED

from *Black Cat Magazine*

My first day at work, Liliana warned me about Brittany. I was sifting through a rack of women's tops looking for misplaced sizes. "You have to watch what you say around her."

I wanted to ask more but the manager was nearby and watching us. Liliana must have noticed too because her body tightened and she walked away.

During lunch, I was eating a sandwich and some cut up vegetables I'd brought from home. Brittany came into the break room and walked straight over to me to shake my hand; she had a firm grip. She settled into a chair across the table. She had luscious hair and a slim sleek body.

"First job?"

"No." I said chewing.

"So, where'd you work before?"

"Dental office."

"Why'd you leave?" Her questions were jarring.

"Different reasons. Anyway, I hope this one sticks."

"Sticks." She said the word the same time as me. "I think you'll do just fine here."

She walked to the vending machine, got a water bottle and skipped out. Later, a man brought a shirt without a tag or receipt. I told him I couldn't refund it.

"Then why are you even here?" he said, his voice rising. I explained the policy but he just got angrier. I looked around and didn't see the store manager anywhere. Brittany finished with her customer and slid over to my register. She leaned down and met the man's eyes. Moving her head close to his, she said, "Sir, we cannot do this."

The words, they were the same as mine; but with hers, he calmed down. He shook his head slowly, took his shirt and left. Brittany put her hand on the small of my back. "Remember, they're not angry at you, they are angry through you." She reached over and grabbed the unopened water bottle from her station. "Let the words wash off."

"Thank you. I always feel like I'm doing something wrong."

The next shift, Brittany and I had our lunch scheduled at the same time. I was microwaving my leftovers when she walked in and sat down at the table. "You eating?" I asked.

"Nah, I had a big breakfast." She waited while I finished warming my food, then said, "I was thinking of you yesterday, of the first day of work and of first days. It reminded me of my first day of kindergarten. My mother came in to dress me, but it was still dark and we didn't turn on the lights since my siblings were sleeping in the same room. We rushed to school; she kissed me on the forehead and sent me on my way. The kids were looking at me strange and I thought it was because I was different. Finally, one girl came up and told me my shirt *and* my pants were inside out." Brittany released a belly-filled laugh and I joined her.

"That happened to you?"

"It happened!" she said. Her whole demeanor was warm and inviting. "Do you have something?"

"That actually reminds me of a story my dad told me. When he first came to this country, he bought this vest but the tag was on the side, folded towards the front, instead of in the back. He'd never seen this, so he thought that this was some kind of new trend where you wore it the other way around, with the zipper in the back."

"No!" Brittany shrieked.

"Luckily, a friend alerted him before he'd gone too far in public. But he likes to say that it looked pretty good that way."

Brittany leaned forward, biting the bottom of her lip. "That story is just delicious."

That evening, I stopped by the grocery store and as I was checking out, I heard a guy in the next aisle talking about wearing a vest backward. I paid and turned around to see who it was, but he was gone. I went home and felt some stomach cramps so I ended up just warming up some broth and going to sleep.

When I saw Brittany at work, I told her what happened.

"Was it your dad?"

"No, he was home."

"Maybe it's a story doppelgänger!" she said. "And we all have one."

Except, I heard it again while I was waiting for the bus. A couple was walking by and the woman talked about a backwards vest. I was about to stop her, but then I felt a rumble in my stomach. I ran to a nearby coffee shop and was relieved to find there were no codes or locks on the door. I made it to the toilet just in time. It felt like there was an earthquake in my intestines.

A few days later, Brittany asked if I wanted to have drinks after work. We met at a nearby pub and she ordered a couple of shots and brought them to the table. "The stomach stuff was pretty bad?" I nodded. She took a shot and pushed one toward me. "When I was a kid, I had to self soothe when I would get sick. My mom, she was stern and treated me like a nuisance. Once, I got so sick, but I was still afraid to tell her. I swallowed down phlegm and coughs for a week. Turned out I had pneumonia."

"That happened to you?" Her mother sounded different from before.

"It happened!" She said and took another shot. "Now your turn."

"I heard someone talk about the vest again."

"That's not a story," she said, and threw her hands back.

"But, don't you think it's strange?"

"Ok fine, you got me. It's possible I told a few people. It was just so funny."

"But I meant it for you."

“Growing up my nickname was Big Mouth Brittany. Don’t tell Brittany or she’ll tell.” I must’ve been making a face because she added, “I’m sorry. I’ll be more careful. Come on, what’s the worst that you’ve been sick?”

The second shot warmed me. “Ok...fine, I didn’t get sick much as a kid. But I did get hurt. My brother used to throw my jump rope on the roof when he got mad. I was pretty agile, and I figured out how to climb the side of the wall and get to the top. Pretty soon it became a game, and I got bolder. I would hang off the side of the house and jump down. The last time, I landed wrong and cracked my ankle.”

“Ouch!”

“First time going to the ER and getting a cast. That was the end of my daredevil years.”

Brittany looked at me with bright eyes. She was loving the story.

Later, the shots must have gotten to me because I was puking all night. I went to work worn and sluggish. Brittany smiled at me from her register; she looked upbeat and well-rested. She reached up her hands as if she was hanging and then collapsed her head and body down to the counter and fake-laughed. I didn’t think it was funny but maybe I was just hungover.

By mid-afternoon, I’d heard two sets of people talk about falling from the roof. I confronted Brittany in the break room. “It’s not okay for you to keep telling people my story.”

“Stories are meant to be shared, otherwise we’d starve.” She spoke calmly, barely looking at me.

I turned around and walked out of the room. My stomach was so upset, I had to ask to leave early. I wasn’t working the next two days, but noticed that Liliana was—it seemed like we had alternate schedules. I went to the store and waited outside. She came out and walked around the corner and lit up a cigarette. She saw me and waved me over. “You look weak; it’s happening, isn’t it?”

"Something is." I shared the last few interactions I'd had with Brittany. "Now I hear my stories everywhere."

"And you get sick after?" I nodded. "It's what she does."

"How?"

"I don't know." Liliana's fingers shook as she held her cigarette. Her phone beeped. "Look, I'm really sorry, my break is up. Just... don't tell her anything."

That week, all of my and Brittany's lunches were at the same time. She came up to me in the break room and asked me how I was feeling.

"Fine."

She waited, clicking her tongue. "You don't want to share something?"

"No, sorry, I'm just really into this book."

"Come on."

"Maybe later?" I shifted in my chair and went back to reading. The following lunch, I went for a walk outside. The third day, I was stocking shelves when the manager called me in. He was the one who had trained me after I was hired. He was years younger, probably a recent graduate, with a pleasant, if bland, demeanor. He told me he was impressed with my performance.

"Tell me more about your work over the last few years."

I shared with him how I managed the entire front team at the dental office, including scheduling and supervision. I wanted him to know that I could take on more responsibilities. He waited for me to say more. "The crash happened, so many places shut down and people just didn't have money for teeth. I did what I could after—driving, shopping, different gigs. I'm just so grateful to have this job."

When I finished, he burped.

My stomach twisted and a putrid taste rose in my throat. I was sick that night.

Liliana and I sat outside at a coffee shop. She took a huge drag from a cigarette and then said, "I first noticed it after 2016. But I think it's something that's been around for a long time."

"It's not just Brittany."

"No, it's spreading and it's getting worse."

"We have to stop it," I said.

"I'm not sure how."

"What if we make up stories?"

I took the bus home and noticed a woman scanning the passengers as she licked her lips. The next day I told Brittany a fake story, and she looked at me strange. "No, that doesn't work, tell me something else." I was flustered and told her I needed to go outside to get some fresh air. Two men were walking by, and I heard one of them telling a story. It had a familiar sound to it. I think it was the story of the vest, but it sounded different. Distorted, almost, as if it were in tatters.

That afternoon, the manager called me in again. He told me he was getting complaints that I wasn't being sociable. "You have to talk to your coworkers."

I really needed this job.

At the end of my shift, Brittany stopped me as I was leaving the store. She hovered over me. "Come on, tell me a story." She held out her palms, face up with her fingers curled into a "come here" gesture. I felt so angry, but the rage got stuck in my throat, and I couldn't get it out. "The boss has spoken, hand it over."

My voice cracked and I felt like I was out of breath. That happened when my emotions were bigger than my words and I couldn't say all that was inside of me. I pushed back tears and told her about how my grandmother was a teacher in the village, but she joined a group of women and they created an underground radio station that would spread news about the fight for independence. The ball in my throat cleared and I felt free, but then my stomach turned and I ran to the bathroom.

Lilliana and I thought we could try and withhold stories. I wasn't scheduled for a few days, so I stayed at home, quiet. I felt some life come back to me, but then it was followed by a feeling of bloat. It got really bad and hurt in a different way. Liliana came to check in on me and I told her a story and felt a release. We started to share with each other but then, after a round or two, we'd bloat up again. We needed more people, people like us.

We walked the streets looking for others. We would see someone gaunt and blanched, leaning against a pole or puking on the sidewalk. We brought them into our story circle. And then we realized, there were so many more, and our circles expanded across the city.

At work, Brittany waited for me all wide eyes and tongue hanging, and I'd spit out a story for her. By now, the physical pain was familiar, the feeling of my guts being all chewed up. But then I'd run to a story circle and the blood in veins would hum again.

The story eaters must've figured it out, watching us getting stronger even when we spilled our insides to them. They alerted the authorities who created the Story Oversight Taskforce. The City Council held an emergency meeting and outlawed all group storytelling. Only one-on-ones and only in public. Stories must be told for consumption.

"But we'll die," we protested. Because when the stories circulated for too long, they would lose their core, unravel and turn into disjointed sounds. After awhile, they were just grey noise, lacking any texture or range, and our people were disappearing.

After the raids, we started to fade. We no longer recognized each other on the streets. I kept giving Brittany my stories until I had none left in me. I settled down at the bus stop and put my head down. It was the end.

I heard a voice but the words were thick and muffled. Someone put a hand on my back and whispered my name. I looked up and searched my mind for a memory until it came. It was Liliana. She put her fingers to her lips, shaking her head slightly. She took my hand and walked me to a car. We drove out of the city and into the mountains. Liliana turned off a single dirt path, and headed deep into the woods. We parked and walked on a trail until we reached an opening. There, a group of people sat me down in front of a fire. Someone got me some warm tea and something to eat. Once I was comfortable, they told me the story of how they first arrived. For days, they didn't know what to do because they had forgotten. Their limbs were weak and their head foggy and there were no words left inside of them. So, they listened to the blue jays calling out to each other, and the owls hooting and the wind howling, and they remembered.

The redwoods hovered above me, swaying with the brisk winds, and I felt protected.

I noticed a tingle in my throat, and I pushed and pushed until I could form a word, and then many came forward. I told them the story of my aunt who remembered the time before they divided up our country. She described how all her classmates were of different religions but they all went to school together. They teased each other but they were friends. And then, she told me how they started to disappear. She said: "One by one, I'd wake up and another house was empty, another family gone in the middle of night."

The blood rushed to my cheeks. I looked around and recognized the faces from our circles. I joined them during the trips to the city to find more people. We watched as life came back into their hands and their lungs filled up with air. But we knew we couldn't live in the mountains forever because that meant we only spoke in fear.

We went back to our homes and continued whispering to each other. We found there were some that didn't eat our stories. And, there were things we didn't understand—how it was that there were more of them than us, or how they would continue to keep feeding if we continued to disappear. And, we chose not to starve them, because then we would be just like them. So, we told them stories and we fed each other even more. We knew that somewhere, sometime, the stories would break this, and so we never stopped.

Loyalty Oath: Dia de los Muertos, November 2020

by MARISOL CORTEZ

I pledge allegiance to birds
and Black birders
I pledge allegiance to sea turtles
and silly gulls
I pledge allegiance to yard sales,
plate sales, voguing, ancient foraging
circuits: nuez, tuna, nopal, yuca
All the gifts of this land
we once wandered, not lost
like Cabeza de Vaca, but logically
seasonally ecologically
moving. I pledge allegiance
to dewberries growing on the banks
of the lake the Army Corps made
from dammed up river
and the red hornets
who live there too, whose protective sting
to my brow while foraging
sends me reeling,
falling
backwards with the force
of a strike

I pledge allegiance to sacred springs
I pledge allegiance to every wetland
and swamp that hid runaway slaves
and Native boarding school children.
May every effort to drain you
fail, may we fill you up again
instead, restore you, so that no
White House built beneath the lash
may comfortably occupy
your Potomac slough.

I pledge allegiance to rivers
that swallow up
ill-gotten walls and
the lies that built them
I pledge allegiance to the burning forests—
Amazonian, ancient redwood
and all alveoli everywhere:
from Floyd's breath extinguished
beneath boot and badge
on a hot Minneapolis sidewalk
to the breaths of elders artificially inflated
by ventilators down in the RGV:
I pledge allegiance to all lungs, all breath,
arboreal or mammalian, Aeolian
winds of the body which
resist just by inspiring
exhaling
surviving

I pledge allegiance to dogs and frogs
and bikes

I pledge allegiance to the 594,000
and counting
the pandemic dead who died over Zoom
When I started this poem
on the eve of first debate
that number was 213,000
Still, we cannot forget
this has happened before
in San Francisco, New York,
San Antonio, the abandoned
dead of the earliest years of AIDS
and so
I pledge allegiance to the love and rage
of the late Larry Kramer
I pledge allegiance to trans kids
and gay TikTok, to the schizophrenic homeless
on the back stoop of Starbucks
to the red-tailed hawks that swirl over
downtown despite

the disappearances of development
and redevelopment

I pledge allegiance to the intelligence
of pigs and corvids, the crows and grackles
who never forget a face

I pledge allegiance to the wonder of thriving
coral reef
taller than the Empire State Building itself
and the discovery there of *Spirula spirula*,
never-before-seen squid
whose shell is internal,
a ram's horn coiled
inside gelatinous body,
posterior glowing
bioluminescent green
like Halloween
glo-stick

I pledge allegiance to poetry,
public libraries, senior centers,
daycare workers, mail carriers,
city pigeons, palaterias, tamaladas,
Food Not Bombs, Bayard Rustin, the rust
that claims the excavator, the sugar in
the gas tank, the microbiome that
makes our bodies mere perturbation
in the flora and forest of bacterial
pluriverse

I pledge allegiance to los chimuelos,
the youngest and oldest among us and
to the memory that persists when the body fails
and the self-organizing joy
of the toddler, moving
nonlinearly through parking lots

I pledge allegiance to the autochthonous
to sage and copal, to the four directions
to the red road, the eight fold path,

to the dream, to Dreamtime, to
Dreamers with a capital-D and
democracy lowercased

to the silence of witness

to the struggle
to the struggle
the upraised fist
but also to the softness
and stillness of the open
hand that knows
no enmity, no homeland
no loyalty

We do this because the world we live in is a house on fire and the people we love are burning.

Sandra Cisneros

CONTRIBUTORS

With roots in the Philippines and Romania, **Amanda L. Andrei** is a playwright hailing from Virginia/Washington D.C. and currently residing in Los Angeles. Her plays are epic, irreverent, and medicinal – she hopes you leave the theatre feeling like you have been in ceremony. Say hi at www.amandalandrei.com.

Karin Aurino writes poetry and fiction. Her work appears or is forthcoming in *Red Rock Review*, *North Dakota Quarterly*, *Sou'Wester*, *Literary Orphans*, *The Satirist*, and elsewhere, and has received recognition from *Glimmer Train*. Aurino lives in Los Angeles with her husband, two children, and their dog, George.

Dinah Berland is the author of two chapbooks: *Fugue for a New Life*, winner of the Watersedge Poetry Chapbook Contest (2020) and *Hotel at the End of the World* (Finishing Line Press 2021). She is currently writing a screenplay based on her nonfiction book, *Hours of Devotion* (Schocken, 2007).

Cynthia Alessandra Briano is Director of the Rapp Saloon Reading Series and Founder of Love On Demand Global. She is the daughter of Mexican immigrants and grew up in Southeast L.A. She earned a BA from Swarthmore College and an MFA from University of California Riverside.

Deborah Edler Brown was born in Brazil and raised in Pittsburgh. Winner of the Sue Saniel Elkind Poetry Prize, Deborah's work has appeared in numerous publications, and her fiction has been twice nominated for the Pushcart. She resides in Los Angeles, where she dances and teaches.

Cecilia Caballero is an Afro-Chicana single mother, poet, creative nonfiction writer, and educator based in Los Angeles. She has received fellowships from Tin House, Macondo, and the Authentic Voices program from the Women's National Book Association and her writing appears in *Dryland, Raising Mothers*, and elsewhere. Twitter @la_sangre_llama.

Lisa Eve Cheby, a librarian, poet, and daughter of immigrants, holds an MFA from Antioch and an MLIS from SJSU. Her poems, essays, and reviews have appeared in various journals and anthologies. Her chapbooks, *Love Lessons from Buffy the Vampire Slayer* and *Buffy Averts a Mid-life Apocalypse* are available from Dancing Girl Press. Visit her at lisacheby.wordpress.com.

Jules Chung (she/her) writes poetry and fiction. Her work appears in *Quince Magazine, The Lumiere Review*, and *Armstrong Literary* and is forthcoming in an anthology in the United Kingdom. She lives in New Jersey and is at work on a novel about Korean immigrants and marriage.

Lisbeth Coiman is a poet and educator from Venezuela. Her debut book, *I Asked the Blue Heron: A Memoir* (2017) explores the intersection between immigration and mental health. Her poetry collection, *Uprising / Alzamiento* (Finishing Line Press 2021) teaches us that uprisings are almost always necessary on the path toward a more just world. Coiman lives in Los Angeles, CA. Visit her at www.lisbethcoiman.com.

Marisol Cortez is a creative writer and community scholar rooted in San Antonio, Texas. She is the author of *Luz at Midnight* (FlowerSong Press, 2020) and *I Call on the Earth* (DoubleDrop Press, 2019), among other poetry, prose, and scholarship. Visit mcortez.net for complete list of publications and projects.

Angela M. Franklin is a writer, poet, and documentarian from Los Angeles, California. A recent MFA graduate from Antioch

University Los Angeles, she volunteers with Pongo, a poetry-writing project for teens in juvenile detention. Poems of witness and social justice are her passion and muse, which are reflected in her work.

Elizabeth Galoozis's work has appeared in *Sundog Lit*, *RHINO*, *Phoebe*, and *Sinister Wisdom*, among others. Her poem "Cento: Six Women in Five Parts" was nominated for a Pushcart Prize. She works as a librarian and lives in southern California. She can be found on Twitter and Instagram @thisamericanliz.

Tanya (Hyonhye) Ko Hong is a poet, translator, and cultural-curator, championing bilingual poetry and poets. Internationally published, she is author of five books, including *The War Still Within* (2019). Her poetry appears in *Rattle*, *Beloit Poetry Journal*, *Entropy*, *Cultural Weekly*, and *WSQ: Women's Studies Quarterly* (The Feminist Press), among others.

In a former life, **Christina Howell** was a project manager, living the American dream. In 2018, she quit her job, sold her house, and boarded a plane to Scotland. After 30 months of travel, she settled in Munich, Germany where she leads an online writing community for memoirists.

Gerda Govine Ituarte is the author of four poetry collections. Her work was published in domestic and international publications and she read in such venues. She established the Pasadena Rose Poets in 2016 and was Editor of their first poetry collection in 2019. She earned an Ed.D. from Columbia University.

Toni Ann Johnson's short fiction and essays have appeared in *The Emerson Review*, *The Los Angeles Times*, *Hunger Mountain*, *Callaloo*, and elsewhere. A novel, *Remedy For a Broken Angel*, was published in 2014 and received a 2015 NAACP Image Award nomination for Outstanding Literary Work by a Debut Author.

Lois P. Jones is the author of *Night Ladder* (Glass Lyre Press). Awards include the 2018 Lascaux Prize, 2017 Bristol Prize judged by Liz Berry and as winning finalist in the 2018 Terrain poetry contest judged by Jane Hirshfield. She has work forthcoming in *Plume* and *Guernica Editions*.

Bonnie S. Kaplan is a poet and educator. She has worked with adults in re-entry for over two decades. Her poems have been published in numerous journals and anthologies including *Sinister Wisdom* and *Adrienne Rich: A Tribute Anthology*. She thrives in Altadena, California. See more at bonnieskaplan.com.

Cybele Garcia Kohel is living and writing in Pasadena, California. Born in Puerto Rico, she writes poetry, fiction, and essays in a loud voice from the margins,in support of many BIPOC issues. She is a mom, a fierce dog lover, and an aspiring librarian.

Elline Lipkin's first book, *The Errant Thread*, was selected by Eavan Boland for the Kore Press Book Award. Her second, *Girls' Studies*, explores girlhood in the United States. A Research Scholar with UCLA's Center for the Study of Women, she teaches for Los Angeles Writing Workshops and recently served as Poet Laureate of Altadena.

VK Lynne is a writer/musician from Los Angeles. Her work includes award-winning web series *Trading on 15*, novels *Even Solomon* and *A Pook is Born*, and poetry chapbook, *Crisis*. In 2016, she was granted a Jentel Arts Residency for creative writing.

Sakae Manning's storytelling centers on alliances and intersectionality amongst womxn of color. Their work gives voice to defiant women and lives in *The Tahoma Literary Review*, *Carve Magazine*, *Dryland*, and *Blood Orange Review*. Manning was writer-in-residence at The Annenberg Community Beach House, a 2019 Summer Fishtrap Writing Fellow, and is a contributing fiction editor for *Barren Magazine*.

Roberta H. Martínez is an actor, writer, director, and historian. She grew up in East LA and is a founding member of The Collective Voz, a playwright's group. Recent works include: *La Ventura, Real Women Wear Masks,* and *the Pan Dulce Trilogy*. She is the author of *Latinos in Pasadena.*

Suzanne C. Martinez's work has appeared in *The Hong Kong Review, Streetlight Magazine, Flash Fiction Magazine, The Broadkill Review,* and others. *The Broadkill Review* nominated her for a 2019 Pushcart Prize and 2020 The Best of the Net Anthology. *Flash Fiction Magazine* has nominated her for a 2021 Pushcart Prize.

Kate Maruyama is the author of the novel *Harrowgate*, the novella *Family Solstice*, and short work featured in numerous journals and anthologies. She writes, teaches, cooks, and eats in Los Angeles where she lives with her family.

Jenise Miller is a mother, urban planner, and writer from Compton. Her writing about Compton, Watts, and growing up in LA's Black Panamanian community is featured in her chapbook *The Blvd*, as well as in the *LA Times, LA Review of Books, KCET Artbound*, and *Boom California*, amongst others.

Ashunda Norris is an award-winning filmmaker, feminist, arkivist and poet living in Los Angeles. Born and raised in the heart of rural, red clay Georgia, the artist loves hot water cornbread, obscure cinema, star gazing, the ocean and celestial Sirius. Link her at ashunda.com.

Tricia Park is a violinist, writer, and creator of the *Is it Recess Yet? Confessions of a Former Child Prodigy* podcast. Tricia is a Juilliard School graduate and received her MFA at SAIC. Her writing appears in *Cleaver* and *FNews*. Tricia is a Fulbright Grantee in Korea.

Natalie Smith Parra's work has appeared in *Creative Nonfiction, Calyx, Mommy Wars*, a Random House anthology, and *Dove Tales*. She has been in residence at Hedgebrook, Mesa Refuge, and Dorland Mountain Arts. "Eviction Blues" was originally published in and nominated for a Pushcart Prize by *Dryland*.

Alixen Pham is an emerging poet. Her work is published or forthcoming with *New York Quarterly, Salamander, Gyroscope Review, diaCRITICS* and *Brooklyn Poets* as Poet of the Week. She leads the Westside Los Angeles chapter of Women Who Submit.

Thea Pueschel is an emerging nonbinary writer and artist. Thea was the winner of the TAEM Flash Fiction Summer 2020 Contest. Thea has been published in *Short Edition, Abstract Elephant*, and *DNA Magazine*.

Luivette Resto, a mother, teacher, poet, and Wonder Woman fanatic, was born in Aguas Buenas, Puerto Rico but proudly raised in The Bronx. Her two books of poetry *Unfinished Portrait* and *Ascension* have been published by Tía Chucha Press. Some of her latest work can be found in *Bozalta* and *The North American Review*. Her third collection is forthcoming from FlowerSong Press.

Lucy Rodriguez-Hanley is a creative non-fiction writer, filmmaker, and mother of two. A Dominicana via Washington Heights now living in Long Beach, California. She is a VONA fellow and is on the board of the Long Beach Literary Arts Center. Her films and writing can be found at www.lucyrodriguezhanley.com.

Alexandra Sheckler lives in Los Angeles, where she works in publishing. Her writing has appeared in *The Sun*.

Joan Seliger Sidney is Writer-in-Residence at the University of Connecticut's Center for Judaic Studies and Contemporary Jewish Life. Her books include *Body of Diminishing Motion: Poems* *and a Memoir, Bereft and Blessed,* and *The Way the Past Comes Back.* Her flash essay, "I Married a Mathematician," appeared in *Fast Funny Women.*

Laura Sturza is an essay, news, and opinion writer, working on the memoir, *How I Got Married After 50 for the First Time.* Her work has appeared in *The LA Times, Washington Post,* AARP's *The Girlfriend, LA Weekly,* and elsewhere. She wrote and performed a one-woman show about house sharing.

Saba Waheed's work has appeared in *Water~Stone Review, The Southeast Review* (Pushcart-nominated), *Bellingham Review, Lunch Ticket,* and others. She was a Caldera 2020 Artist-in-Residence. She co-produces the podcast *Re:Work* and is the research director at the UCLA Labor Center using research as a tool to elevate community stories.

Romaine Washington is the author of two collections of poems, *Purgatory Has an Address* and *Sirens in Her Belly.* She has presented her work in a wide variety programs including NPR, National Poetry Slam, and KPFK. Washington is a fellow of The Watering Hole, South Carolina.

Aruni Wijesinghe is a project manager, ESL teacher, erstwhile belly dance instructor and occasional sous chef. She has solo collections forthcoming in 2022 with Moon Tide Press and Silver Star Laboratory. She lives a quiet life with her husband Jeff and her cats Jack and Josie.

Hazel Kight Witham is a mother, educator, slam poetry coach, and writer trying to summon a little peace every day. She can be read in *The Sun, Bellevue Literary Review, Mutha Magazine,* and *ACCOLADES: A Women Who Submit Anthology.* Learn more about her at www.hazelkightwitham.com.

Sandy Yang's fiction has appeared in *Santa Monica Review, The Los Angeles Review, Juked, South Dakota Review*, and elsewhere. Her story collection was named a semi-finalist for the Iowa Short Fiction Award, and she was awarded a Tennessee Williams Scholarship to the Sewanee Writers' Conference.

The author of the critically acclaimed literary novel *The Amado Women*, a sampling of **Désirée Zamorano**'s writing has appeared in *Catapult, Cultural Weekly*, and the *Kenyon Review*. She is a frequent contributor to the *LA Review of Books*. Pummeled by contemporary events, for this story she wanted to write the world right.

Nicole R. Zimmerman (MFA, University of San Francisco) was a 2019 recipient of Creative Sonoma's Discovered Awards for Emerging Literary Artists. Her work appears in literary journals including *Creative Nonfiction* and *The Rumpus*. She lives with her wife in Northern California where she leads writing workshops. Learn more about her at www.nicolerzimmerman.com.

EDITORS

Fiction Editor **Ryane Nicole Granados** is the Chapters Director for Women Who Submit. She is an AWP featured presenter and has attended the Bread Loaf Writer's Conference in Sicily, Voices of Our Nation Arts, and the Community of Writers at Squaw Valley Workshop. She is a Los Angeles native whose writing finds its roots in her love of community and her belief that Black motherhood is an act of social justice. She is inspired to write stories of survival that magnify the marginalized while also unearthing the splendor of second chances. Her storytelling has been showcased in the national stage production Expressing Motherhood and KPCC's Live Series Unheard LA. Her novella *The Aves* is forthcoming with Angels Flight Books. She earned her MFA in creative writing from Antioch University Los Angeles.

Fiction Editor **Lorinda Toledo, PhD** is a mestiza/Chicana feminist from New Mexico who has lived in Los Angeles for over a decade. Her novel-in-progress was named first runner-up for the 2019 James Jones First Novel Fellowship. Her short fiction has been published in the *Mississippi Review, The Normal School,* and elsewhere. Lorinda earned a doctorate in Literature with Creative Dissertation from the University of Nevada, Las Vegas in 2019, where her work was supported by a Black Mountain Institute Fellowship and other awards. Her MFA is in fiction and creative nonfiction from Antioch University Los Angeles. Recently, Lorinda became an acquisitions editor for Jaded Ibis Press. Previously, she was fiction editor at *Witness* literary magazine. Lorinda teaches writing at Antioch University Los Angeles and is a writing coach and editor. Learn more at lorindatoledo.com.

Creative Nonfiction Editor **Noriko Nakada** is the Blog Managing Editor for Women Who Submit. She is a multi-racial Asian American creative who strives to capture the hidden stories she has been told not to talk about. Her essay, "A Short History of Insanity," appeared in *Meridian*. She has published three book-length memoirs: *Through Eyes Like Mine*, which was shortlisted for the 2040 Book Award, *Overdue Apologies*, and *I Tried*. Excerpts, essays, and poetry have been published in *Made in LA*, Vol. 3, *Hippocampus*, *Catapult*, *Linden Avenue*, and elsewhere. She completed her MFA at Antioch University Los Angeles and teaches English in a Los Angeles public middle school. She is on Twitter @writersgrind.

Creative Nonfiction Editor **Flint** is a queer writer with an abiding interest in hybridity, generative genre tampering and upsetting the applecart of heteronormative discourse about sex/uality. She earned an MFA in Writing from the School of Critical Studies at CalArts, and her work has appeared in *CutBank* (All Accounts & Mixture), *Erotic Review*, *Arts & Letters* (Unclassifiable Contest winner), *NAILED Magazine*, and *Staging Social Justice* (Southern Illinois University Press), among other publications and anthologies.

Drama Editor **Xochitl-Julisa Bermejo** is co-founder and Executive Director of Women Who Submit. She serves as WWS's liaison to Exposition Park Branch of the Los Angeles Public Library and other community organizations. She is WWS's primary grant writer. She has presented on submission strategies at the National Latinx Writers' Gathering, Macondo Writers Workshop, Hugo House, BinderCon, and other places. Her poetry collection, *Posada: Offering of Witness and Refuge*, was published by Sundress Publications in 2016. She earned a creative writing MFA from Antioch University Los Angeles and teaches creative writing through UCLA Extension, Antioch University, and Writing Workshops LA; she is also a community arts educator.

Drama Editor **Sharnell Blevins**'s voice encompasses everything she is, settled within her soul. She exhibits this in her writing of plays, poetry, short stories, and novels which are showcased on stage, literary journals, and readings. She has an MFA from Mount Saint Mary's University and was an Editor of *The Rush Literary Journal.* She is a member of the Association of Writing Professionals and Programs, Dramatist Guild, Kite City Playwrights, New Play Exchange, and Playwright's Center. Sharnell lives in the Los Angeles area with her husband, Clifton, and their six children. Her website is: sharnellblevins.com.

Poetry Editor **Lauren Eggert-Crowe** is the Special Events Coordinator for Women Who Submit. Her primary role is to support and publicize our programming efforts. She has also presented on submission strategies at a UCLA Extension class and has co-presented Women Who Submit history at BinderCon 2016. Lauren Eggert-Crowe is the author of four poetry chapbooks, including *Bitches of the Drought*, which was selected as a finalist in the Sundress Publications 2016 Chapbook Competition. She has an MFA in poetry from The University of Arizona.

Poetry Editor **Lituo Huang** is a Chinese-born, Midwest-bred, and Los Angeles-based writer of fiction and poetry. She is the author of a chapbook of short fiction and poetry, *This Long Clot of Love.* Her work has appeared in *TriQuarterly*, *Dryland*, the *VIDA Review*, and elsewhere. She was a former assistant fiction editor at *JMWW*. You can find her at www.lituohuang.com and on Twitter @LituoH.

Managing Editor **Tisha Marie Reichle-Aguilera** is the Website Manager for Women Who Submit and curates the calendar of calls for submission. She has presented on submission strategies at the National Latinx Writers' Gathering, Macondo Writers Workshop, and the Latina Writers Conference. A Chicana Feminist and former Rodeo Queen, she writes so the desert landscape of her childhood can be heard as loudly as the urban chaos of her adulthood. She is obsessed with food. Her stories have appeared most recently in *Emerge Literary Journal, Peatsmoke, SCARLET: A Literary Blog, The Coachella Review Daily,* and the anthology *Puro Chicanx Writers of the 21st Century* (Cutthroat and Black Earth Institute). She has been an editor for *Border Senses, VIDA Review,* and Ricochet Editions. A former high school teacher, she earned a creative writing MFA from Antioch University Los Angeles and is a PhD candidate in creative writing and literature at University of Southern California where she is an Annenberg Fellow.

WWS LEADERSHIP TEAM

Xochitl-Julisa Bermejo, *Executive Director*

Tisha Marie Reichle-Aguilera, *Website Manager*

Lauren Eggert-Crowe, *Special Events Coordinator*

Cybele Garcia Kohel, *Fundraising Coordinator*

Noriko Nakada, *Blog Managing Editor*

Ryane Nicole Granados, *Chapters Director*

Lucy Rodriguez-Hanley, *Chapters Liason*

Sakae Manning, *Social Media Managing Editor*

FOUNDERS

Alyss Dixson

Ashaki M. Jackson

Xochitl-Julisa Bermejo

Where there is a woman there is magic. If there is a moon falling from her mouth, she is a woman who knows her magic, who can share or not share her powers. A woman with a moon falling from her mouth, roses between her legs and tiaras of Spanish moss, this woman is a consort of the spirits.

Ntozake Shange

ABOUT THE ORGANIZATION

Women Who Submit is open to all women and nonbinary writers. Our mission is to empower writers and encourage submissions to literary journals, residencies, and fellowships. Each quarter, the Los Angeles-based organization hosts workshops and submission parties where we support one another with claps and cheers. You can view past offerings on the **Workshop Archive** page of our website or on our YouTube channel. Membership is free.

We promote our mission, future projects, and public events through our social media channels.

FOLLOW US

Twitter/IG @WomenWhoSubmit
facebook.com/women who submit
YouTube: Women Who Submit Los Angeles

To find a chapter in your area or for information about how to create a Women Who Submit chapter in your area, visit the **Join Us** page.

To learn more about our organization and meet our leadership team, visit the **About WWS** pages.

CONTACT US

womensubmit@gmail.com

womenwhosubmitlit.org

www.ingramcontent.com/pod-product-compliance
Lightning Source LLC
Chambersburg PA
CBHW070351200726
48294CB00003B/841

* 9 7 8 1 7 3 3 2 4 1 5 4 0 *